DATE DUE

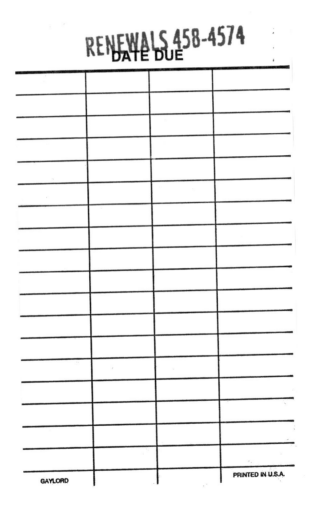

SCARECROW PRESS, INC.

Published in the United States of America
by Scarecrow Press, Inc.
A wholly owned subsidiary of
The Rowman & Littlefield Publishing Group, Inc.
4501 Forbes Boulevard, Suite 200, Lanham, Maryland 20706
www.scarecrowpress.com

PO Box 317
Oxford
OX2 9RU, UK

British Library Cataloguing in Publication Information Available

Library of Congress Cataloging-in-Publication Data

∞™ The paper used in this publication meets the minimum requirements of American National Standard for Information Sciences—Permanence of Paper for Printed Library Materials, ANSI/NISO Z39.48-1992

Contents

Preface

In the winter of 1982, I arrived in Tunis to embark on a period of eighteen months field work for my doctoral thesis on the Arab musical tradition known as *al-mūsīqā al-andalusiyya,* or *al-maʾlūf* (literally, "familiar," "customary"). Little did I know, as I enrolled in my Arab music solfège class at the national conservatory, a gracious colonial-style edifice on the Avenue de Paris, that this was to be the start of a relationship with a country, a musical repertory, and its personalities that would continue to absorb me for the following two decades, drawing me repeatedly back to Tunisia to refine, update, expand upon, and redirect my original inquiry.

I had chanced upon the *maʾlūf* some three years earlier on a visit to the island of Djerba, close to the border with Libya, where I had heard the traditional melodies sung by Jewish cantors adapted to Hebrew words. My *ᶜūd* (Arab lute) teacher Habib Gouja identified their melodic modes and rhythms; later, on my return to England, he sent me extracts of the *maʾlūf* transcribed into Western staff notation, set to Arabic texts, and essays on the history and theory of the *maʾlūf,* taken from publications by the Ministry of Culture. From Habib's missive, I learned that, since the 1930s, the entire repertory had been transcribed from oral tradition into Western staff notation for use in teaching and performance; after independence in 1956, the Ministry of Culture had published and promoted the notated canon throughout the country as a unitary, national tradition.

It was this information that shaped my original inquiry. I wanted to know more about the relationship between the notated canon and the oral traditions that preceded it; whether the same traditions were continuing alongside the notated versions; and whether musicians outside the state musical establishment considered the notated canon to represent a unitary, national tradition. I was interested to discover the background and circumstances surrounding the original notation project and its adoption by the newly independent government. More broadly, I was curious to know the status of the traditional repertory in relation to the newer ones promoted by the mass media.

This book presents key aspects of my research on the *maʾlūf* since 1982. Like the related Arab musical traditions of Morocco, Algeria, and Libya, the *maʾlūf* was allegedly imported to North Africa by Andalusian refugees—Muslims and Jews fleeing the Christian reconquest of Spain from the tenth to the seventeenth centuries. Ultimately, the *maʾlūf* is derived from the Arabo-Persian music that developed in the early Islamic courts of Damascus and Baghdad. This music spread westward, in the wake of the Arab conquests, into North Africa and Spain, where it developed its distinctive Andalusian traits. The *maʾlūf* thus shares music structural principles, terminology, instruments, performance conventions, and a written theoretical and philosophical heritage with a vast complex of Arab, Persian, and Turkic musical repertories spanning a geographical area from northwest Africa through the core Middle East to Central Asia.

This is the first book in the English language on Tunisian music, or on any other national tradition of *al-mūsīqā al-andalusiyya,* and it is the only book in any language to survey changes in the Tunisian tradition, since its modern revival in the early twentieth century, within the framework of social, political, and musical developments in Tunisia and the wider Middle East. In it, I explore such topics as Arab musical aesthetics; modernization, Westernization, and Egyptianization; the use of notation in oral tradition; musical nationalism and cultural policy; ideologies of national, regional, and individual musical identity; concepts of "art" and "popular," and relations between traditional music and the mass media, whose significance extends beyond Tunisian and Middle Eastern music to ethnomusicology as a whole.

In the first chapter I introduce the *nūba*—the principal genre of Arab Andalusian music. I take as my starting point a quotation from the Tunisian scholar and musical connoisseur, Manoubi Snoussi, comparing the aural effect of the *nūba* to the visual effect of an Arab garden. After presenting the *nūba* in its historical and social context, I describe the musical and poetic characteristics of the Tunisian genre according to the terms and concepts of contemporary Tunisian music theory. Then, focusing on a performance of *nūbat al-sīka,* widely available on compact disc, I explore the symbolic associations of Snoussi's analogy and I identify the music structural qualities underpinning the aesthetic effects he describes. My discussion is based on a complete musical transcription of *nūbat al-sīka* with the Arabic song texts in transliteration and English translation.

The second chapter is devoted to the Baron Rodolphe d'Erlanger, patron, amateur performer, and pioneering scholar of Arab music, best known in academic circles as the author of the monumental six-volume work *La Musique Arabe* (1930–1959). Scion of an aristocratic banking family of German-Jewish extraction, d'Erlanger produced this work in Tunisia, where he lived from 1911 until his death in 1932. Supported by entourage of local musicians and scholars, d'Erlanger turned his home– the magnificent Moorish palace *Ennajma Ezzahra* ("Resplendent Star"), into a center of Arab musical performance and scholarship. Drawing from d'Erlanger's writings and the oral accounts of Tunisians, I describe the traditional social contexts for the *maʾlūf,* d'Erlanger's observations on its current state of decline, and his ideology and vision for its future. I then consider d'Erlanger's contributions, as both patron and scholar, to the modern renaissance of the *maʾlūf;* in particular, his role in laying the foundations of modern Tunisian music theory, educational methods, and institutional patronage.

In chapter 3 I recount how, in the wake of d'Erlanger's project, the Rashidiyya Institute was founded in Tunis with the aim of preserving and promoting traditional Tunisian music. In its attempt to standardize the diverse versions of the melodies passed down in oral tradition, the Rashidiyya transcribed the entire repertory of the *maʾlūf* into Western staff notation for use in teaching and performance. Far from crystallizing the melodies into one standard version, however, the Rashidiyya's original transcriptions provided the impetus for successive layers of prescriptive notations reflecting the different ideologies and aesthetic preferences of subsequent leaders of the ensemble. I illustrate their contrasting approaches in a comparison of five notated versions of the same song.

Chapter 4 focuses on the effects of state cultural policy on the *maʾlūf* of Testour, a historic center of the tradition, following Tunisian independence in 1956. In its attempt to present the *ma᾽lūf* as a unitary national tradition, the Ministry of Culture published the Rashidiyya's transcriptions in a series of nine volumes entitled *al-Turāṯ al-mūsīqī al-tūnisī (The Tunisian Musical Heritage),* which it distributed to newly established state-sponsored music educational and recreational institutions throughout the country. Despite the government's claim to the contrary, however, the people of Testour insist that they possess a distinctive *ma᾽lūf* tradition, which they have made a conscious effort to preserve. I examine the conflicting claims of the Ministry of Culture and the musicians of Testour in a comparison of three versions of a song, performed or transcribed in Testour between 1960 and 1983, with the published version.

In chapter 5, I consider the changing relations between the *ma᾽lūf* and new composition following the rise of the mass media in the early twentieth century. Tunisians describe the *ma᾽lūf* as the "cradle" of Tunisian song: over the centuries, new compositions inspired by the traditional melodies, latterly reflecting broader Middle Eastern influences, were integrated anonymously with the old. In the early twentieth century, however, the increasing vogue for Egyptian and new varieties of Tunisian song, stimulated by the emerging record industry, was perceived by some as a threat to the *ma᾽lūf.* In response, the Rashidiyya ensemble, bastion of the traditional repertory, provided the platform for top media stars to perform new popular songs by the Rashidiyya's composers. After independence, with the assimilation of the *ma᾽lūf* into the government's cultural and educational program and the founding of the state radio ensemble, a gulf was created once more between the *ma᾽lūf* and the new, predominantly Egyptian-inspired songs promoted by the mass media.

In chapter 6 I present five projects representing alternative approaches to the *ma᾽lūf* and its related repertories that emerged or acquired renewed prominence in the aftermath of the Tunisian *coup d'état* of July 11, 1987 known as *"al-Taġrir"* ("The Change"). Typically, the alternative approaches embody ideals of authenticity and/or personal expression, and their recent blossoming is associated with new directions in Tunisian cultural policy favoring decentralization and the dismantling of unitary nationalist agendas. My examples feature high-profile musicians and singers in Tunis from the 1990s to the present.

Much of the material presented here has been published previously in various formats, scattered over a wide range of sources, not all of which are equally accessible. This book represents an attempt to gather together this wide spectrum of interrelated topics, expanding upon and updating them where appropriate, in such a way as to reveal their chronological and thematic relationships. Chapter 6 is based closely on my article in *Music and Anthropology* 7, *Journal of Music and Anthropology of the Mediterranean* (2002). I thank the editor, Tullia Magrini, for her permission to reproduce this material.

This is not the full story of the *mā'lūf:* after more than twenty years, my research is still ongoing. During this time, my story has touched upon other, closely related repertories that cry out for further exploration, yet which I can only allude to here. I refer in particular to the popular media genre *al-uġniya al-tūnisiyya* (literally, Tunisian song), introduced in Chapter 5, whose development ran parallel with the *ma'lūf* through the early decades of the twentieth century. These songs were fostered by the Rashidiyya and cultivated by composers, singers, and instrumentalists steeped in the *ma'lūf,* yet their relationship with the traditional repertory remains largely unexplored. This topic is the focus of a current project continuing from Mourad Shakli's ground-breaking study on *La Chanson Tunisienne* (1994).

My research has, by its very nature, depended primarily on knowledge, information, ideas, and experience provided freely by others. It would be impossible to thank personally so many who, for so long, welcomed me, initially as a stranger, into their musical lives and contributed to my work with their generosity, their time, their patience, and, above all, their passion for their music. Yet there are some whose contributions have been pivotal, whether to this work in particular or to my project as a whole. Foremost among these are Habib Gouja, who introduced me to the *ma'lūf* and gave me the information I needed to initiate this project, and Salah el-Mahdi, who welcomed me into the Tunisian musical establishment, provided the initial framework for my studies, and continued to offer his support, when needed, throughout my research. Among others whose input dates back to my first field trip (in 1982–83) I am particularly indebted to Abdelhamid Belalgia, Amor Baouab, Hadj Mohamed Ben Ismail, Hamadi Bougamha, Abdelkadir Boushaba, Baroness Edwina d'Erlanger, Dr. Belhassan Farza, Mongi Garouachi, Tahar Gharsa, Ahmed Hamrouni, Hedi Horrigue, Shaykh Abdelrahman el-Mahdi, Rashid Sellami, Mohamed Saada, Mohamed Triki, and Fethi Zghonda. On subsequent visits my work has been enriched immeasurably by my encounters with Anouar Braham, Lotfi Boushnak, Mahmoud Guettat, Mounir Hentati, Sonia M'Barek, Mourad Shakli, Beshir Soussi, Amina Srarfi, and Hatem Touil.

My initial field work would not have been possible without the generous support of a fellowship awarded jointly by the Social Science Research Council (U.S.) and the American Council of Learned Societies (funded by the Ford Foundation and the National Endowment for the Humanities). Subsequent field trips were funded by the University of Cambridge Travel Fund and research grants from Corpus Christi College, Cambridge.

My work has benefited over the years from the invaluable feedback and encouragement I have received from my teachers, students and colleagues. I thank in particular Stephen Blum, Philip Bohlman, Cheryl Frances-Hoad, Frank Ll. Harrison, Jehoash Hirshberg, Morris Kahn, Tullia Magrini, Roger Parker, Harold Powers, Kathryn Stapley and Martin Stokes. I am grateful to Kim Burgess for his ingenuity and patience in transcribing the musical examples and song texts onto computer; to Jill Furmanovsky for her inspiration and ideas for the cover design; to Mustafa Ja'far for creating the Arabic calligraphy for the cover; and to Kathryn Stapley for her transcription, transliteration and translation of the *ma'lūf* texts. Finally, I thank Sam Grammer and his team at the Scarecrow Press for their enthusiasm, efficiency, and care.

Note

Arabic words are transliterated according to the system used by the *International Journal of Middle Eastern Studies* with the following exceptions:

i For people's names I use the forms they use themselves, if known. Otherwise, in the case of Tunisian names, I use forms commonly adopted by Tunisian sources. In other cases, I use the standard system. When quoting from published sources I use the forms given.
ii Place names and other well-known words (e.g., shaykh) are left in their familiar forms.
iii Songs texts transcribed from recordings reflect the forms as sung. These may differ from the forms given in published sources.

In describing musical pitches I use uppercase letters for pitches below middle c, lowercase letters for the octave ascending from middle c, and single primes for pitches above this octave.

The musical examples adopt the pitches conventionally used for the *maqām* in question. These do not necessarily correspond to the actual pitches performed.

Chapter One

The *Nūba* and the Arab Garden

In the notes to his record *The Classical Andalusian Music of Tunis* (FW 8861) Wolfgang Laade quotes from a conversation with the distinguished Tunisian musical connoisseur and scholar, the late Manoubi Snoussi.[1] In advising how best to appreciate this music, Snoussi drew the analogy with an Arab garden, enclosed by a circular wall, laid with lawns and flowers, its paths all leading towards a central pavilion, open to all sides:

> There I will stand and look around. I may turn to this side or that and the view will always be the same. There is nothing irregular, nothing disturbing my mind. And . . . everything comes towards me. I am able to allow it to come or not, according to my mind, I can accept or refuse. There is nothing disturbing or alarming me. Thus it is with our music.
>
> (Laade 1962: 3)

In this chapter I use Snoussi's analogy as a backdrop for my discussion of the *nūba*, the principal large scale form of Arab Andalusian music. I focus on *nūbat al-sīka*, the main item in Laade's collection, performed by the Rashidiyya ensemble led by Salah el-Mahdi in Tunis, in 1960. First, I introduce the *nūba* in its historical and social contexts in North Africa; then, focusing on el-Mahdi's example, I describe the particular musical and poetic characteristics of the Tunisian *nūba* according to the terms and concepts of contemporary Tunisian music theory. Finally, returning to Snoussi's analogy, I consider the symbolic associations of the garden and I identify the musical criteria underpinning the aesthetic effect he describes.

THE NORTH AFRICAN *NŪBA*

The *nūba* is the characteristic large-scale form of the Arab music of the Maghreb, or western Arab world, spanning Morocco, Algeria, Tunisia and Libya. Known generally as *al-mūsīqā al-andalusiyya*, this music is believed to have been imported to North Africa by so-called Andalusian refugees—Muslims and Jews fleeing the Christian reconquest of Spain from the tenth to the seventeenth centuries.[2] Today, *al-mūsīqā al-andalusiyya* is divided into various national and regional traditions known as *āla* (instrumental music) in Morocco, *ṣanᶜa* (work of art) in Algiers, *ġarnāṭī* (from Granada) in Western Algeria, and *ma'lūf* in Eastern Algeria, Tunisia and Libya. United by their common Andalusian identity, these traditions share certain music structural and linguistic characteristics, and aspects of performance practice, which distinguish them as a whole from the music of the Arab east, or Mashreq.

The origins of a distinctive Arab-Andalusian musical tradition date back to the early ninth century when the outstanding musician ᶜAlī ibn Nāfī, known as Ziryāb (a freed Persian slave) was ousted from the court of Baghdad by his jealous teacher and rival Isḥāq al-Mawṣilī. Turning westward, Ziryāb eventually found refuge in the court of ᶜAbd al-Raḥmān II in Cordoba. There, he founded a music conservatory in which he developed new compositional principles based on a system of twenty-four melodic modes, or *ṭubūᵓ*.

Each *ṭabᶜ* was associated with particular cosmological and other properties including hours of the day, natural elements, colors of the spectrum, and human emotional and physical attributes, and each had corresponding therapeutic properties. Many of these associations are still acknowledged by North African musicians, even if they are no longer respected in practice. Ziryāb also defined rules for the sequencing of different song types, progressing from slow/heavy rhythms to fast/light ones, thus sowing the seeds of the characteristic progression of the North African *nūba*.

From the tenth century, waves of Muslim and Jewish refugees fled into North Africa, concentrating in towns in the northern and coastal regions. The first migration, from the 10th to the 12th centuries, was from Seville to Tunis; in the twelfth century, refugees fled from Cordoba to Tlemcen (Algeria) and from Valencia to Fez (Morocco); then, with the fall of Granada in 1492, a further wave of migrants made for Fez and

Tetuan (Morocco). There is a popular belief that the differences between the various contemporary North African traditions still partly reflect this original pattern of migration from Spain, where each city allegedly cultivated its own rival school of Andalusian music. The imported repertories continued to develop, through centuries of oral transmission, along separate lines in their host countries, resulting in the four distinct national traditions known today.[3]

The *nūba* is essentially a song-cycle characterized by unity of mode, or melody type, and diversity of rhythmic-metric elements. The song texts belong to the literary forms of *qaṣīda* (in classical Arabic), *muwaššaḥ* (in a mixture of classical and dialectical Arabic) and *zajal* (in dialect alone). Both music and words have survived in oral tradition, but the song texts were also recorded in special collections called *kunnāšāt* (s. *kunnaṣ*, note-book) in Algeria and Morocco, and *safāʾin* (s. *safīna*, vessel) in Tunisia and Libya. Their themes are typically romantic descriptions of love, wine and nature whose meanings were traditionally exploited, particularly in Sufi contexts, for their ambiguity: love may be both worldly and divine, nature has heavenly associations, and wine could be the elixir of paradise.

Each *nūba* is named after the particular mode, or *maqām* (pl. *maqāmāt*), to which its repertory belongs. This comprises a core stock of precomposed vocal melodies, each representing a particular rhythmic-metric genre or *iqāᶜ* (pl. *iqāᶜāt*). The term *nūba* is used to denote both the system of classifying these melodies and the principle of organizing them in performances. In the first sense, all the melodies belonging to a particular *maqām* are arranged in a standard sequence of *iqāᶜāt;* in the second, a variable number and selection of the melodies are performed in the same rhythmic-metric sequence. Other types of repertory may be added, including instrumental pieces in different *iqāᶜāt*; all performances, however, must preserve the characteristic sequence of the core *iqāᶜāt*.

The term *nūba* is conventionally translated as suite. In my discussions with Abdelhamid Belalgia, director of the Tunisian radio ensemble, he proposed an alternative definition, arguing that as a system of both selecting and ordering repertory, the *nūba* is analogous rather to a program. The crucial difference, he explained, is that the contents of a suite are fixed, while those of a *nūba* may vary in substance, type, and duration from one performance to the next.[4]

As an urban tradition, the *nūba* has been exposed to various foreign influences, notably Turkish since the sixteenth century, and both Egyptian and European from the late nineteenth century.[5] Historically it has enjoyed elitist, even aristocratic patronage: in Morocco the Alawite Sultan Muḥammad ben ᶜAbd Allah (d. 1790) and his son Mulāy ᶜAbd al-Salām (d. 1822) commissioned the famous treatise and authoritative *kunnaṣ̌*, *Majmū'at al-Ḥāyik* (c. 1800), while in Tunisia, Muḥammad al-Rašīd Bey (1710–59) is credited with the current organization of the *nūbāt* and with the composition or commissioning of the instrumental pieces (Guettat 2000: 248–9; 303).

But the *nūba* is fundamentally a popular tradition. Until the advent of modern state patronage and the parallel decline of the Sufi movement, its chief patrons and exponents were Sufi brotherhoods: popular religious organizations where orthodox Islamic taboos against musical activity were waived and the dichotomy between art and popular culture resolved. Outside the Sufi lodges, *nūbāt* were performed by professional musicians in coffee houses, sometimes accompanied by hashish smoking, and in communal celebrations for religious and family festivals such as weddings and circumcisions. The anonymous, timeless melodies were familiar to all: they belonged to the community, they were performed for and by the community, they were part of the communal heritage.

THE TUNISIAN *NŪBA*

In the first two decades following independence, the melodies of the Tunisian *ma'lūf* were transcribed in Western staff notation and published by the Ministry of Culture in a series of nine volumes entitled *al-Turāṯ al-mūsīqī al-tūnisī—Patrimoine Musical Tunisien (The Tunisian Musical Heritage)*. The transcriptions were edited by Salah el-Mahdi, director of Music and Popular Arts. According to el-Mahdi they were based on those originally produced by the Rashidiyya Institute, founded in Tunis in 1934 with a mission to conserve and promote traditional Tunisian music.[6] Volumes 3–8, dedicated to the thirteen *nūbāt,* provide the notated sources for my discussion of the Tunisian *nūba.* [7]

The Vocal Cycle

The Tunisian *nūba* comprises a core cycle of five vocal genres called *bṭāyḥī* (pl. *bṭāyḥiyya), barwal* (pl. *brāwil), draj* (pl. *adraj*), *xafīf* (pl. *xafāyif)* and *xatam* (pl. *axtam*). A sixth, the *dxūl al-barwal* is considered

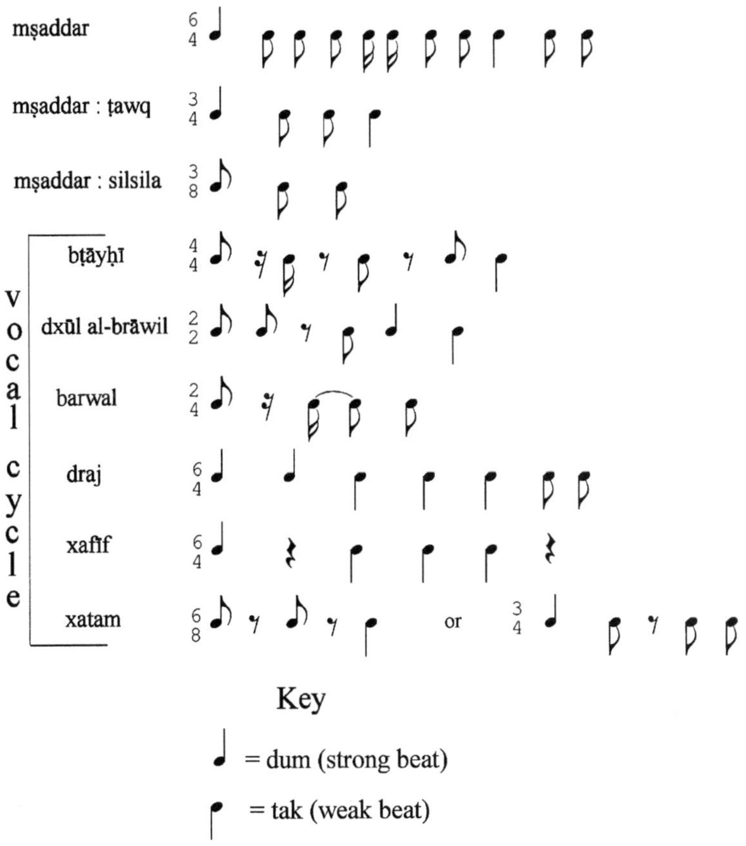

Example 1. The **iqā'āt *of the Tunisian* nūba *(el-Mahdi n.d.a: 16)***

a derivative of the *barwal,* which it precedes in five *nūbāt* (see Table A on p. 11). Each genre is named after its corresponding *iqā*^{c} as shown in Example 1.

The thirteen *nūbāt* are themselves arranged and conventionally performed in a particular order (see Table A below), thus forming a macrocycle based on a fixed sequence of *maqāmāt*.

The vocal cycle falls into two sections: the first in duple meter and the second in triple meter. Each section proceeds from slow to fast and from longer to shorter rhythmic cycles producing overall an alternating rather than a progressive sequence.[8]

The Structure of the Songs

The song texts belong to the poetic genres of *muwaššah* and *zajal;* the *muwaššah* combines classical Arabic and dialect, the *zajal* uses dialect alone. Both genres adopt a similar formal principle in which two types of strophe, *bayt* (pl. *abyāt*) and *qufl* (pl. *aqfāl*) alternate, ending with the *qufl*. Each strophic type is independent in its number of lines, meter, and rhyme scheme; however, the rhyme of the successive *abyāt* is variable, whereas that of the *aqfāl* remains constant. The *qufl* thus functions as a type of refrain.

The melodies generally follow the strophic form of the poetry in a predominantly repetitive manner. Normally only two strophes are included, a *bayt* followed by a *qufl*; if more strophes are added, the melodic setting remains the same as for the original pair. The *bayt* typically contains three lines and the *qufl* two, although again, this pattern is variable. Each line of the *bayt* is set to the same melody with instrumental repetitions between the lines. The first line of the *qufl* usually signals a new melody, or a variant of the main melody, called the *ṭālaᶜ* (literally, departure). The *qufl* closes with a return to the original melody, the *rujūᶜ* (literally, return), as illustrated:

	verse rhyme	melody	
	A	a (a)	
bayt	A	a (a)	
	A	a	
qufl	B	b or a′ or a	*ṭālaᶜ*
	B	a	*rujūᶜ*

Ensembles and Performance Practice

The typical performance practice of the Sufi brotherhoods is called *maᵓlūf xam* (literally, "raw" or "unrefined" *maᵓlūf*); This is characterized by a male chorus singing in unison accompanied by hand clapping and/or percussion such as the *darbūka* (vase-shaped drum), *naqqārāt* (pair of small kettle-drums), *bandir* (frame drum with snares on the underside), or *ṭār* (tambourine). Each *firqa* (musical group) is directed by a shaykh, normally an elderly member chosen for his superior knowledge of the repertory. The shaykh is responsible for teaching the songs to the rest of the ensemble, controlling the tempo, and leading the transitions from one piece to the next. In *maᵓlūf xam* the five or six vocal genres constitute the complete *nūba* cycle.

In some towns, notably Tunis, the *maᵓlūf* is traditionally performed outside Sufi circles by ensembles that include melody instruments. Until the 1930s, such ensembles typically comprised a *rabāb* (spike-fiddle with two strings), sometimes replaced by a violin in repertory other than the *nūbāt*, an *ᶜūd ᶜarbī* (short-necked North African lute with four strings), *naqqārāt, ṭār*, and one or more solo singers; the instrumentalists doubled as chorus. In the 20th century, under the influence of Egyptian ensembles, instruments such as the *ᶜūd šarqī* (short-necked lute with five or six strings), *qānūn* (plucked zither), and *nāy* (bamboo flute without mouthpiece) were sometimes used, as well as Western instruments of fixed pitch, such as the harmonium and the mandolin.

The shaykh of the instrumental ensembles normally played either *ᶜūd* or *ṭār*. Like the shaykh of the Sufi *firaq* he provided the authoritative melodic renderings; however, each solo instrumentalist and singer was free to interpret these in an individual way, embellishing them spontaneously according to his personal taste and the natural articulation of his instrument or voice. The result was a variable, heterophonic texture.

In the mid-1930s, the Rashidiyya Institute created a new, enlarged type of ensemble that has since become standard throughout Tunisia (see chapter 3). While the exact lineup is variable, the basic model comprises several violins, two or three cellos, one or two double-bass (usually played pizzicato), *darbūka*, *ṭār*, and *naqqārāt*, an arbitrary smattering of traditional Arab melody instruments such as the *ᶜūd ᶜarbī*, *ᶜūd šarqī*, *nāy*, *rabāb*, and *qānūn* (one or more of each type), and a separate male and female chorus. The instrumental texture is dominated by the bowed strings in unison and octaves; the instrumentalists play from notation and the ensemble is led by a conductor with a baton.

The Expanded Nūba Cycle

In the performance of a *nūba,* the instruments play a variety of roles both supportive and independent of the voices. In the songs, they double the vocal melody and respond with varied repetitions; between songs they link the different genres with short introductions and interludes called *adxal* (literally introductions; s. *dxūl*) and *fāriġāt* (literally, empty, i.e., without words; s. *fāriġa*); and they introduce the vocal cycle with two full-scale instrumental genres, independent of the core *iqāᶜāt*, called *istiftāḥ* and *mṣaddar*. The Rashidiyya added a new vocal and instrumental genre, the *abyāt* (literally, verses), to precede the *bṭāyḥīya* in the same *iqāᶜ*. Finally, in certain *nūbāt,* the instrumentalists interrupt the vocal cycle with a dramatic change of *maqām* in an instrumental diversion called the *tūšiya*.[9]

The *istiftāḥ* (literally, opening) establishes the *maqām* at the start of the performance. According to el-Mahdi, it was "formerly a kind of musical theme on which one of the musicians used to improvise, followed by the rest of the ensemble" (el-Mahdi n.d.a.: 11). Apparently this process disappeared after the themes were notated by the Rashidiyya. The *istiftāḥ* now comprises several broadly flowing phrases of irregular length in duple meter, without rhythmic cycle, played in strict unison by the melody instruments alone, without percussion.

The *istiftāḥ* leads directly into the *mṣaddar*, an instrumental overture in triple meter performed by the whole ensemble, comprising three sections, each in a different *iqāᶜ*: *mṣaddar*, *ṭawq* (literally, necklace), and *silsila* (literally, chain) (see Example 1). The *mṣaddar* proceeds from slow to fast, culminating in the *silsila*, in which a short sequential motive gradually accelerates to a sudden, abrupt halt.

The main section, called *mṣaddar*, is based loosely on the structure of the modern Turkish *peşrev*. This is an instrumental overture in which four sections, or *hane-s* (Arabic: *xānāt*; s. *xāna*) of equal length are followed by a refrain called *teslim*. Each *hane* modulates to a different *makam* or range, returning to the nominal *makam* in the *teslim*. The *mṣaddar* uses the corresponding rubrics *xānāt* and *taslīm*.

However, the modulations in the *xānāt* occur less systematically than in the *peşrev*, there may be fewer than four, and these are not always of equal length.[10] The *ṭawq* and the *silsila* are each based on a sequential repetition of a formulaic pattern that varies little, if at all, from one *nūba* to the next.

Before the founding of the Rashidiyya, it was customary for the solo singer to introduce the vocal section with an improvized genre in free rhythm on a *qaṣāid* (pl. *qasīd* a poetic genre in classical Arabic), called the *abyāt* (el-Mahdi n.d.a.: 11). In the process of transcribing the *nūbāt*, the Rashidiyya transformed the *abyāt* into a fixed composition for chorus and ensemble in *iqā^c al-bṭāyḥī* with an integrated instrumental introduction, or *dxūl*, and interludes called *fāriġāt*.

The *dxūl al-abyāt* is in two sections: the first, in the brisk *iqā^c al-barwal*, provides a transition from the frenzied close of the *mṣaddar* to the stately *iqā^c al-bṭāyḥī* of the second section. The main vocal section is a setting of two lines of classical poetry in *iqā^c al-bṭāyḥī*: the first (bayt 1) is repeated to a different melody and the second (bayt 2) has a new melody again. The three vocal melodies are separated by two contrasting *fāriġāt*, as shown below. The *abyāt* ends with a sudden accelerando.

section	**melody**
dxūl	*a*
bayt 1	*b*
fāriġa 1	*c*
bayt 1	*d*
fāriġa 2	*e*
bayt 2	*f*

The *abyāt* leads directly into the brief *dxūl al-bṭāyḥiyya* (introduction to the *bṭāyḥiyya).* Like the *dxūl al-abyāt*, the *dxūl al-bṭāyḥiyya* proceeds from a fast section in *iqā al-barwal* to a slow section in *iqā^c al-bṭāyḥī;* it thus provides a transition from the accelerated close of the *abyāt* to the stately pace of the following *bṭāyḥiyya.*[11]

The expanded *nūba* cycle is thus broadly divided into an instrumental introductory section followed by a predominantly vocal section. In each part, duple are followed by triple meters, long by short rhythmic cycles, and slow by fast tempi. Following the pattern of the vocal cycle, the overall sequencing principle is alternating rather than progressive:

	genre	meter	rhythmic cycle	tempo
	istiftāḥ	duple	/	slow
instrumental	*mṣaddar*	triple	long	slow
	ṭawq	triple	short	faster
	silsila	triple	short	fast
	abyāt = bṭāyḥī	duple	long	slow
	bṭāyḥī	duple	long	slow
vocal	*barwal*	duple	short	fast
	draj	triple	long	slow
	xafīf	triple	long	slow
	xatam	triple	short	fast

The *tūšiya* is not considered part of the *nūba* proper but rather, a diversion from it. Interrupting the vocal section between the *bṭāyḥīyya* and the *brāwil,* the *tūšiya* is anomalous in belonging to the *maqām* of the following *nūba* in the macro-cycle. It thus functions as a herald for the next performance. Essentially it is a medley of ensemble, solo, pre-composed, improvised, metered and non-metered elements based on a two-part structure proceeding from *iqā*ᶜ *al-barwal* to *iqā*ᶜ *al-bṭāyḥī*. El-Mahdi provides the following description of the *tušiya*:

> It starts on *iqā*ᶜ *al-barwal*; then one musician improvises phrases on the same *iqā*ᶜ and the ensemble repeats the previous section before leading into a section in *iqā*ᶜ *al-bṭāyḥī*. The ᶜ*ūd* player then performs *istaxbārāt*[12] which introduce various *maqāmāt*, sometimes continuing with *sawākit*, namely melodies of popular songs. Occasionally a singer improvises on several verses in literary Arabic before leading into the following *muwaššah* [i.e. the *brāwil*].

Table A shows the number of examples of each genre in each of the thirteen *nūbāt* according to the published canon.

THE TUNISIAN CONCEPT OF *MAQĀM*

In his comparative study of the Tunisian *maqāmāt*, introducing the eighth volume of *al-Turāṯ*, el-Mahdi uses the term *maqām* to designate "the various musical scales [*salālim*; s. *sullām*] underlying the repertory of traditional Tunisian music, known as the *ma*ᵓ*lūf*." He notes that the terms *naġma* in Egypt, *ṣawt* in Saudi Arabia, and *ṭab*ᶜ in the Maghreb, were traditionally used in senses corresponding to *maqām*; however, "with the development of mass media and improved communications,

Table A

	istiftāḥ	*mṣaddar*	*dxūl + abyāt*	*bṭayḥī*	*tūšiyya*	*dxūl al-barwal*	*barwal*	*draj*	*xafīf*	*xatam*
nūbat al-ḏīl	1	1	1	17	1 = ʻirāq	0	9	6	10	3
nūbat al-ʻirāq	1	1	1	10	0	2	5	4	5	2
nūbat al-sīka	1	1	1	5	0	0	3	2	4	3
nūbat al-ḥsīn	1	1	1	8	1 = raṣd	2	11	5	5	6
nūbat al-raṣd	0	0	1	7	0	0	3	4	4	2
nūbat ramal al-māya	1	1	1	8	1 = nawā	1	5	4	5	3
nūbat al-nawā	0	0	1	8	0	1	7	4	5	2
nūbat al-aṣbaʻayn	1	1	1	8	1 = rāst al-ḏīl	0	11	3	5	7
nūba rāst al-ḏīl	1	1	1	9	0	3	7	3	3	3
nūbat al-ramal	1	1	1	11	1 = aṣbahān	0	7	3	5	3
nūbat al-aṣbahān	1	1	1	7	0	0	4	3	3	2
nūbat al-mazmūm	1	1	1	5	0	0	6	2	5	2
nūbat al-māya	1	1	1	6	0	0	10	4	5	4

maqām has become the most widely used term, prevailing over all others of equivalent meaning" (el-Mahdi n.d.b: 17).[13]

The Arab Musical Scale

Each *maqām* scale is derived from a hypothetical general scale of forty-nine named pitch degrees called "The Arab Musical Scale." El-Mahdi presents this, both in notation and as a list of names, as a two-octave scale of 24 quarter-tones (*rubʿ*; pl. *arbāʿ*) per octave ascending from G (*yakāh*) to g' (*jawāb nawā*). In the notated example he uses the standard Arab accidental symbols 𝄳 and ≠ to represent the quarter tone degrees between ♮ and b and between ♮ and # respectively. El-Mahdi's "Arab Musical Scale" corresponds to d'Erlanger's *échelle générale* (1949: 20) and to Marcus's "Modern Arab Scale" (Marcus 1989: 99).[14]

When the 24-tone Arab scale was first introduced in Syria in the latter part of the eighteenth century, it was conceived as equal tempered; however, this notion has since been widely challenged by both theorists and musicians. In Tunisia, as elsewhere in the Arab world, the symbols 𝄳 and ≠ are generally understood to represent alterations of variable degrees depending on factors such as melodic context, national and regional tradition and individual taste. In his transcriptions, however, apart from the illustration of the general scale, el-Mahdi uses the following accidentals to distinguish between three degrees of "half-flat":

𝄳 = lowering of pitch by 20%
𝄳 = lowering of pitch by 30%
𝄳 = lowering of pitch by 40%.[15]

Maqāmāt and *ʿUqūd*

El-Mahdi illustrates the seventeen *maqāmāt* of the *maʾlūf* and their variants in a total of 22 scales ordered according to their "tonic" degree (*darajat al-irtikāz*; literally, "degree of support"). Apart from *maqām al-raṣd*, characterized by a single pentatonic octave, the remaining sixteen *maqāmāt* are "related to those of eastern Arab-Islamic countries based on a set of tonal units [Arabic: *ʿuqūd*; s. *ʿiqd*, literally, necklace] linked together in ascending and descending scales" (n.d.b.: 18).

Example 2 reproduces el-Mahdi's scales of the thirteen *nūbāt* (el-Mahdi n.d.b.: 25–33).

Example 2.   Maqāmāt of the 13 Tunisian nūbāt (el-Mahdi n.d.b.: 23–33)

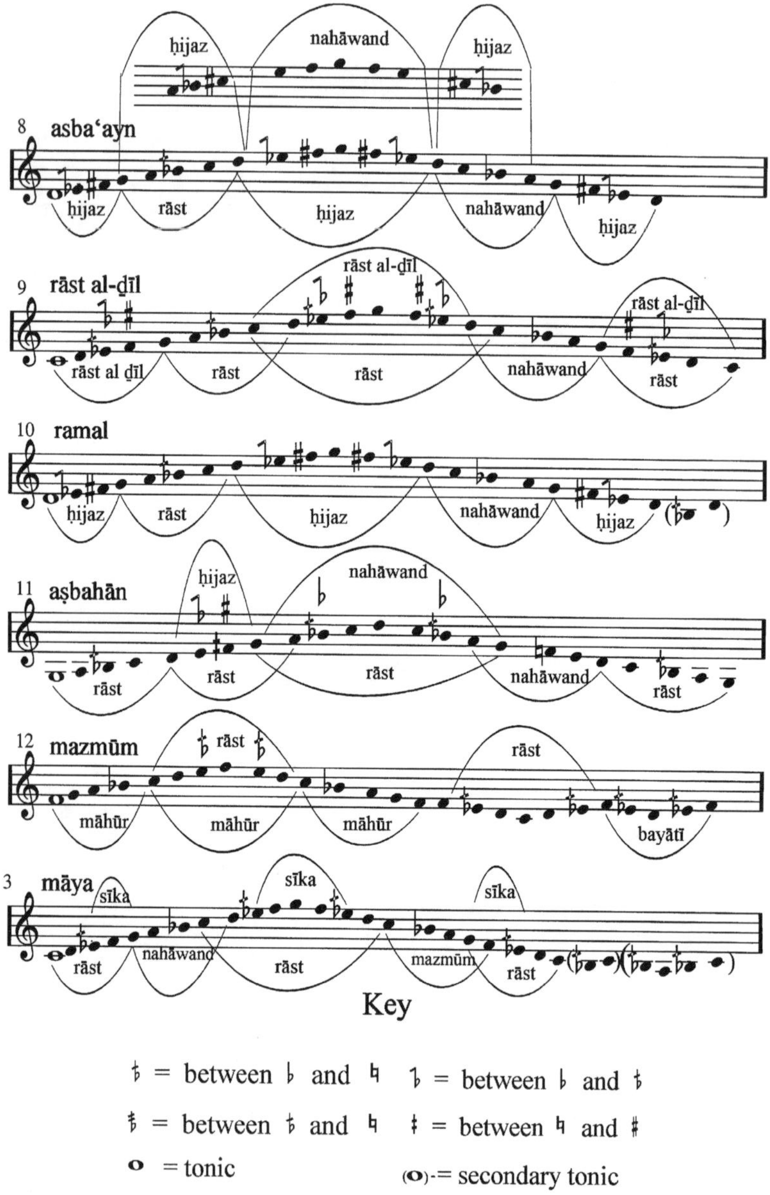

Example 2. continued

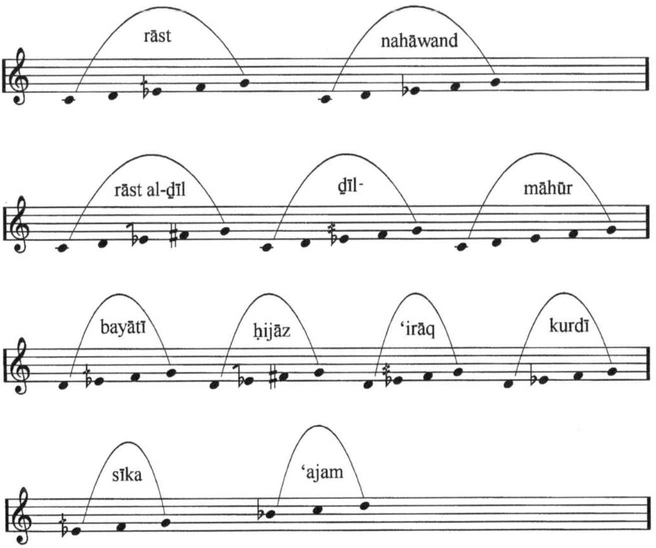

Example 3. The 'uqūd of the Tunisian maqāmāt (el-Mahdi n.d.b.: 25)

Each tonal unit, or *ᶜiqd*, comprises a set of three, four, or five successive scale degrees defined by intervallic structure and root degree. The individual *ᶜuqūd* may be transposed, typically by intervals of an octave, fourth, or fifth (see for example *ᶜiqd al-rāst* in el-Mahdi's scale of *maqām al-sīka*).

Example 3 illustrates the eleven principal *ᶜuqūd* of the Tunisian *maqāmāt*.

El-Mahdi's *maqām* scales typically comprise three consecutive *ᶜuqūd* in each direction; alternative *ᶜuqūd* are shown for most *maqāmāt*. The *ᶜuqūd* are identified within the scales by name and, if transposed, by their initial degree. The ascending and descending scales are not necessarily identical, and the upper octaves do not necessarily replicate the lower

In a commentary beneath each scale, el-Mahdi describes the melodic progression of *ᶜuqūd*, notes certain characteristic melodic features, and draws comparisons with *maqāmāt* of other national traditions. Finally, he illustrates each scale by a short composition identified by *maqām* and *iqāᶜ*.

El-Mahdi's method of presentation, if not its actual content, is clearly modelled on Rodolphe d'Erlanger's exposition of the "oriental" Arab modes in his reports to the 1932 Cairo Congress and in *La Musique Arabe* 5 (pp. 45–47). El-Mahdi acknowledged the influence of both these sources on his work (el-Mahdi n.d.b:18). Curiously, however, el-Mahdi does not refer specifically to d'Erlanger's exposition of the Tunisian *maqāmāt*, included in *La Musique Arabe* 5. These are presented in a considerably more rudimentary manner than the "oriental" traditions that form the main body of d'Erlanger's work.

D'Erlanger presents the "oriental" modes as ascending and descending scales of normally four "genres" (*ᶜuqūd*) in each direction; within each scale the individual genres are identified both by name and by Roman numerals according to their order from the tonic, or root degree. Each scale is followed by a commentary describing the melodic progression of the *ᶜuqūd* and other salient melodic characteristics. Finally, each *maqām* is illustrated by a short "improvization," or *taqsīm (pl. taqāsim)*.

D'Erlanger's Tunisian examples, in contrast, are presented as ascending scales only, comprising two or three *ᶜuqūd*; these are identified by Roman numerals but not, as in the "oriental" examples, by name; nor does d'Erlanger provide any commentary on melodic movement. However each Tunisian scale is illustrated by an *istaxbār* (*"prélude instrumental"*) corresponding to the oriental *taqsīm*.[16]

SOURCES OF *NŪBAT AL-SĪKA*

El-Mahdi's recording of *nūbat al-sīka* was made at a public concert by the Rashidiyya ensemble in Tunis, 1960. Apparently only a random selection of the ensemble was present; it comprised just three violins played by el-Mahdi and two students; two *ᶜūd ᶜarbī* played by Khemais Tarnane and his student Tahar Gharsa; a female "teacher" playing the *ṭār*; three unidentified musicians playing cello, *rabāb,* and *naqqārāt;* and a chorus of predominantly male and some female voices. Apart from the *ṭār* player, the instrumentalists were all men (Laade 1962: 3).

The recording omits the *istiftāḥ* and *mṣaddar* and opens instead with a solo improvisation in free rhythm (*istaxbār*), played on the *ᶜūd* by Khemais Tarnane. This is followed by seven songs: the *abyāt,* a *bṭāyḥī,* two *brāwil,* a *draj,* a *xafīf and* a *xatam,* which together complete the essential cycle of *iqāᶜāt*. The performance lasts approximately 22 minutes.

Until 1992, el-Mahdi's recording remained the only widely available source of the complete vocal cycle of a Tunisian *nūba*.[17] In that year, the Tunisian Ministry of Culture and the *Maison des Cultures du Monde* (Paris) launched a series of recordings entitled *Tunisie Anthologie du Malouf*. Subtitled *enregistrements historiques*, the first four volumes reproduce recordings of *nūbat al-ḏīl*, *nūbat al-ramal*, *nūbat al-ᶜirāq* and *nūbat al-aṣbahān* made by the radio *maʾlūf* ensemble around 1960.[18]

The fifth volume, produced in 1994, is a contemporary recording of *nūbat al-sīka* by a reduced ensemble featuring veteran musicians and singers of both the Rashidiyya and radio ensembles conducted by Fethi Zghonda; the ensemble comprises five violins, *nāy, ᶜūd ᶜarbī, qānūn,* cello, *ṭār* and *naqqārāt* and a chorus of five male and five female voices. In Zghonda's recording *nūbat al-sīka* is represented by nine songs, including the seven recorded by el-Mahdi, and the full range of instrumental genres. It lasts 52 minutes and 30 seconds.

Example 4. Extract from *nūbat al-sīka*

Example 4. **(*continued*)**

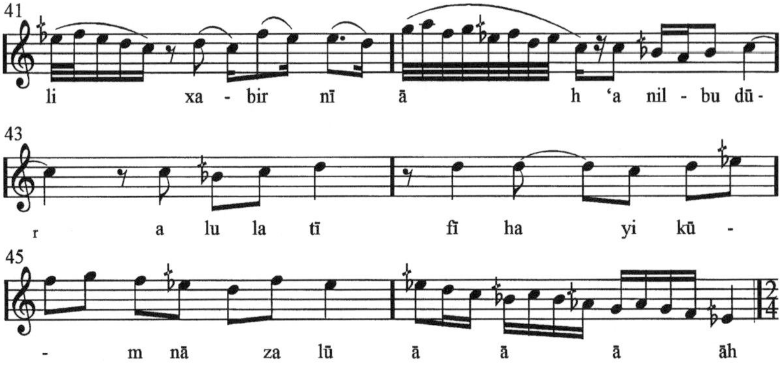

dxūl al-btāyḥiyya

Example 4. (continued)

Example 4. **(*continued*)**

Example 4. (continued)

barwal 2

a - llah lā yaq tā na - ṣīb ha ttā nuqa - bbi-l
tāla‘
wa - j na tū qul lī ‘ā lā - š ba - d dal ta nī
rūjū‘
wa ṣir ta taḥ li - f fi -l ya - mīn lāš yāġ zā - lī
xun ta nī a- llah hasī - bul xā ni nīn

fāriġat al-draj

Example 4. **(*continued*)**

draj 1

fāriġat al-xafīf

***Example 4.* (*continued*)**

xafīf 2

Example 4. **(*continued*)**

xatam 1

Example 4. **(*continued*)**

nūbat al-sīka
(*al-Turāṯ* 5:33-37)

al–abyāt

lammā ‘alimtu bi-anna il-qawm qad raḥlū
wa rāhib ad-dīr b-il-injīl muštaġlu
yā rāhib ad-dīr b-il-injīl tuxbirunī
‘an al-budūr allatī fī ḥayykum nazalū

bṭāyḥī 3

b-ir-rabb allaḏī farraj ‘alā ayyūb
wa baššar b-il-hanā’ yūsuf ma‘a ya‘qūb
ajma‘ yā mawlāī šamlī ma‘a al-maḥbūb

ṭāla‘

li-annī fanīt lammā b-il-hajr manīt
wa al-qalbu yuṣlā bi-nāru

rujū‘

hāḏāka huwwa jazā’
man yabūḥ l-in-nās b-asrāru

barwal 1

ṣāhib al-‘uyūn al-ḥiwara
la–ha ẓaraf wa ma‘ānī
āš ḥāl takūn az-zīyāra
xallī yakūn al-fulānī
rūḥī nahabha bi-šāra
yawman narāh wa yarānī

ṭāla‘

naḥlif yamīn wa anā ṣādiq
maḥbūbī mā ḥiddtu ‘annu

rujū‘

qalbī li-nūr ‘aynī šāyiq
wa al-bu‘du baynī wa baynu

barwal 2

allah lā yaqṭa‘ naṣīb		ḥattā nuqabbal wajnatu
lāš al-ḥabīb yansā al-ḥabīb		mā aṣ‘ab ‘annī furqtu
hadā jazā qalb al-ka’īb		illī ḥaṣal fī ‘ašqatu
	ṭāla‘	
qull lī ‘alāš baddaltanī		wa ṣirta taḥlif fī il-yamīn
	rujū‘	
lāš yā ġazālī xuntanī		allah ḥasību al-xā’inīn

bayt 2

illī ankawā bi-‘uyūn al-aqāḥ		wa ‘aqrab aṣ-ṣudġ wa aš-ša‘r
wa a‘ṭā qalbu l-il-milāḥ		mā yanfa‘ū siwan aṣ-ṣabr
min al-masā ilā aṣ-ṣabāḥ		ṣirtu naqna‘ b-in-naẓar
	ṭāla‘	
hajrak qatalnī wa ‘allnī		wa ṣirta taḥnit fī il-yamīn
	rujū‘	
lāš yā ġazālī xuntanī		allah ḥasību al-xā’inīn

draj 1

mā kāna bīh walā ‘alayh	walā saḥāb fī samāh	rūḥī fidāh
ġarra al-la‘īn iblīs bīh	ḥattā alā al-waṣl qasā-h	zāda fī jafāh
wa ṣirtu mahmā naltaqīh	na‘mal rūḥī mā narāh	lakin āhhh
	ṭāla‘	
b-il-ams kuntu mu‘āniqu		wa al-yawm min waṣlī nafar
	rujū‘	
allah ḥasīb man xallaqu	‘allamū at-tīh wa an-nafār	sulṭān uṣ-ṣaġār

xafīf 2

mā abdaʻa an-nawwār ʻalā šuṭūṭ as-sawāqī
k-aḍ-ḍayā maʻa an-nujūm wa al-laylu bāqī
wa ḥaqqa ʻahid-na wa yawm at-talāqī
anā al-wafī abadan ʻalā al-ʻahd bāqī

ṭālaʻ

nadīmī qum imlā kāsī b-il-ḥamla al-layl jann wa walā

rujūʻ

anā yā ḥabāyib afnānī al-hajrān
ṣaffaf al-qaṭīʻa wa al-kās wa imlā yā sāqī

xatam 1

axaḏa al-aqla wa sār lā hanā walā mazār
mazaq ṯawb al-iṣṭibār wa huwwa ṯawb lā yuʻār

ṭālaʻ

man yurid ʻišq al-milāḥ layluhu yarjaʻ nahār

In 1993, a year after launching the series *Tunisie Anthologie du* Malouf, the Maison des Cultures du Monde issued an innovative recording by the Tunisian media star Lotfi Bushnak, entitled *Malouf Tunisien.* This features Bushnak singing three *waṣlāt,* or abbreviated *nūbat,* including *waṣlat al-sīka,* accompanied by an ensemble of six instrumental soloists. *Waṣlat al-sīka* opens with the *dxūl al-abyāt* leading into a violin solo in free rhythm *(istaxbar)* and a vocal solo with violin responses, also in free rhythm *(inšād).* This introductory section is followed by the *bṭāyḥī, brāwil* and *draj* of el-Mahdi's recording.[19]

Example 4 reproduces el-Mahdi's notations of the seven songs included in his recording of *nūbāt al-sīka,* taken from *al-Turāṯ* 5: 38-49. The Arabic song texts, given here in transliteration and English translation, are taken from *al-Turāṯ* 5*:* 33–37.

nūbat al-sīka

al-abyāt

When I heard about the tribe's departure
I found the monk of the monastery busy with the Gospel
O monk of the monastery, by the Gospel tell me
about the full moons that dwelt in your neighbourhood

bṭāyḥī 3

By God who cured Job and brought happy news to Joseph and Jacob
I beg you, Lord, reunite me with my loved one

tāla‘

Because I wasted away when I experienced the separation
And my heart was branded by its fire

rujū‘

That is the fate of the one who reveals his secrets to people

barwal 1

The one with the beautiful eyes, she has elegance and morals
How long will the visit be? Let it be with so and so

I would give my soul as a token if I could see him and he could see me every day

tāla'

I swear I am telling the truth, I didn't abandon my beloved

rujū'

My heart is longing for the light of my eye
And there is distance between me and him

barwal 2

God doesn't take away one's fate until I kiss his cheek
Why does the lover forget the lover? How difficult is this separation!
My poor sad heart deserves this because it was captured by love

tāla'

Tell me why he dropped me for someone else and he had sworn not to

rujū'

Why, O gazelle, did you betray me? God will punish the betrayers

bayt 2

He who has been branded by the clear eyes, by the round face and the hair
He gave his heart to the sweet one. He has but to be patient
From evening to morning I was content with looking at her

tāla'

Your abandoning me killed me and made me ill. You broke your promise

rujū'

Why, O gazelle, did you betray me? God will punish the betrayers

draj 1

He was fine there's no cloud in his sky. I am ready to sacrifice my soul to him

The cursed devil tempted him. He even made him more cruel about the meeting.
His indifference increased
I began, whenever I met him, to pretend that I hadn't seen him, but ahhh

tāla'

Yesterday I was embracing him and today he fled from me

rujū'

God will punish the one who influenced him. He taught him pride and arrogance.
Sultan of the children

xafīf 2

How wonderful are the flowers on the banks of the brook
Like the light with the stars and the night I remain
I swear by our promise and the day of our meeting
I, the faithful one, will always keep the promise

tāla'

My drinking companion, get up and fill my glass to the brim
The night fell and drew close

rujū'

As for me, dear friends, the separation destroyed me
Line up the flask and the glass and fill, O wine bearer

xatam 1

He took my mind and went and never visited
He tore the dress of patience and it is a dress that isn't ashamed

talā'

The one who wants the love of the sweet one, his nights become days

ASPECTS OF *NŪBAT AL-SĪKA*

Maqām al-Sīka

El-Mahdi acknowledged in our conversations that the versions of the Tunisian *maqāmāt* in *al-Turāṯ* (Example 2) did not always correspond to those given by d'Erlanger. In the case of *maqām al-sīka* there are differences not only between el-Mahdi's and d'Erlanger's scales but also between these and the scale Fethi Zghonda describes in the notes to his recording of *nūbat al-sīka*. The three versions of *maqām al-sīka* are illustrated in Examples 5a, 5b, and 5c. In each example, the *ᶜuqūd* are labelled numerically according to their position in relation to final or root *ᶜiqd*.[20]

In d'Erlanger's single-octave scale (Example 5a), *ᶜiqd* –I (below the final) is represented by the lower trichord of *ᶜiqd al-rāst* (c – e𝄳); *ᶜiqd* I (on the final) by the the trichord *ᶜiqd al-sīka* (e𝄳 – g); and *ᶜiqd* II by the alternative tetrachords *ᶜiqd al-rāst* and *ᶜiqd al-nahāwand* on g.

El-Mahdi's scale (Example 5b), in contrast, is based on *ᶜiqd* I and extends to *ᶜiqd I'* at the upper octave. He thus replaces d'Erlanger's trichord *rāst (ᶜiqd* –I) at the lower octave by the pentachord rāst (*ᶜiqd* –I′ + I′) at the upper octave, in which the embedded trichord *sīka* (*ᶜiqd* I′) is explicitly shown. In his commentary, el-Mahdi draws attention to this entwinement of *rāst* and *sīka* as a defining melodic characteristic of the *maqām*.

Like d'Erlanger, el-Mahdi gives alternative forms of *ᶜiqd* II. In the first form, el-Mahdi represents *ᶜiqd* II by *rāst* in both the ascent and the descent in an arrangement that he describes as "peculiar to the Maghreb" (*al-Turāṭ* 8: 21). Alternatively, *rāst* may be replaced by *ḥijāz*, "yielding the formulation that is commonly called *sīka* in the eastern Arab countries and corresponds also to the mode *huzam*" (*ibid.*).

Nevertheless, there are discrepancies between el-Mahdi's scale and his description of *maqām al-sīka* on the one hand and his transcriptions of *nūbat al-sīka* on the other. In the latter, *ᶜiqd* II is represented by both *rāst* and *nahāwand* but not by *ḥijāz*; certain pieces (the *abyāt*, *dxūl al-bṭāyḥiyya*, *fāriğāt al-draj,* and *draj*) include an additional form of *ᶜiqd* II characterized by the interval a𝄳–𝄳; and in the *abyāt* a𝄳 –b also occurs. All four varieties of *ᶜiqd* II occur in the second setting of *bayt* 1.

a). D'Erlanger's scale of sīka (d'Erlanger 1949: 346)

b). El-Mahdi's scale of sīka (el-Mahdi n.d.b. : 30)

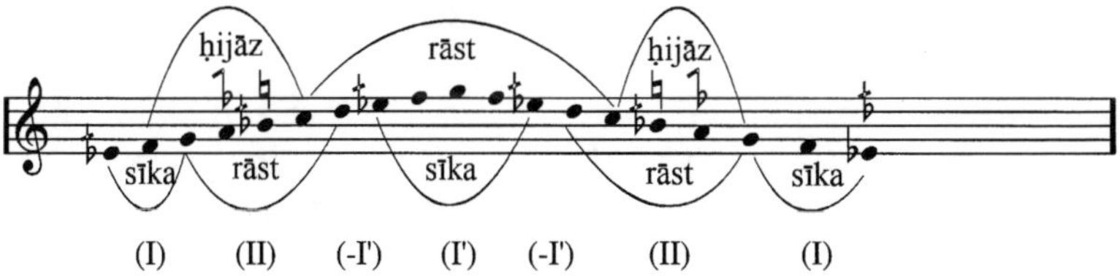

c). Zghonda's scale of sīka (Zghonda 1994: 15-16)

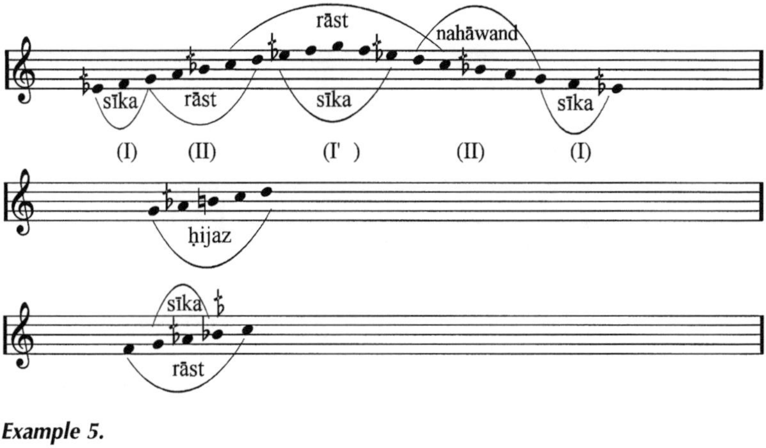

Example 5.

Zghonda's scale (Example 5c) spans the same ambitus as el-Mahdi's, and he too notes the presence of the *sīka* trichord embedded in the *rāst* pentachord on c in the upper octave (^{c}*uqūd* –I' and I'). ^{c}*Iqd* II is identified as *rāst* on g in the ascent and *nahāwand* on g in the descent. However, Zghonda continues, 'the originality of this mode in this *nūba* is due to the fact that this same tetrachord (^{c}*iqd* II) may also be transformed into *sīka* or *ḥijāz* on G and into *rāst al-ḏīl* on F in the descending movement and that these modulations can be intermingled" (Zghonda 1994: 16). According to Zghonda's description, therefore, the interval a𝄳–𝄳 in el-Mahdi's transcriptions of *nūbat al-sīka* should be interpreted as *sīka* on g and the interval a𝄳–b as *rāst* on f.

To summarize, all three sources present the *sīka* trichord embedded in the upper part of the *rāst* pentachord, whether in the lower octave as ^{c}*iqd* I or in the upper octave as ^{c}*iqd* I'. ^{c}Iqd II is highly variable: it occurs in a total of five different forms. Of these, only two are represented by d'Erlanger and all five by el-Mahdi and Zghonda. In the case of el-Mahdi however, only four appear in his transcriptions of *nūbat al-sīka*; the fifth, *ḥijāz* on g, appears in his scale alone.

2 Ambitus, Melodic Direction, and Cadences

Except for the *abyāt,* whose ambitus extends upward through *rāst* on c′, the songs span a uniform range of approximately c – c′ (i.e., ^{c}*uqūd* –I, I and II) as shown in d'Erlanger's scale.

The inherent ambiguity between the degrees *rāst* (c) and *sīka* (e𝄳) produced by the trichord c – e𝄳 below the final is manifested in certain pieces by melodic gravitation towards and repeated phrase endings on c. See, for example, *barwal* 1, where the opening four-measure theme descends sequentially through the *rāst* pentachord to c; on subsequent repetitions, the phrase is rounded off by an ascent to the final. The *xatam* opens with a repetition of a four-measure phrase outlining *rāst,* beginning and ending on c.

Each piece and, with just three exceptions, each section cadences on the final e𝄳. The exceptions occur in the *ṭāla*^{c} (by nature contrastive and transitional) of *barwal* 2, the *draj,* and the *xafīf,* which close on g, d, and c respectively.

In the *barwal*, the melodic context, emphasising e𝄳 and the *sīka* trichord, and the compressed time scale counteract the effect of the momentary gravitation away from the final. In both the *draj* and the *xafīf*, in contrast, the irregular cadences of the *ṭāla*^{c} are consistent with a general melodic gravitation to c.

The *bayt* of the *draj* outlines an arch from c through c' back to c; the cadential phrase on the final in measure 5 appears as though tagged on as an afterthought. The first two measures of the *tala*,' based on the second phrase of the *bayt*, descend through rāst from g to c. It is an abbreviated version of this phrase, closing on d, that leads into the *rujū*^{c}.

The *bayt* of the *xafīf* comprises six two-measure phrases closing on g c c c c and only finally, on e𝄳. The *ṭāla*^{c} restates the last two phrases of the *bayt*, both now closing on c, followed by a third phrase closing on c. The *rujū*^{c} then restates the cadential sequence of the *bayt*.

Cadences on the final are marked by two melodic types. The first type ascends from the third below via the second above the final (c–f–e𝄳) as at the close of both sections of the *dxūl al-abyāt*, mm. 6 and 12. The second type is based on a stepwise descent to the final, as at the end of all three sections of the *bṭāyḥī*. This frequently includes a turn between the third and fourth degrees above the final (g–a–g–f–e𝄳) as at the close of *fāriġa* 1, m. 12.

Melodic Repetition, Variation, and Contrast

The melodic structure of the songs is inherently repetitive (p. 6). This is reinforced by a tendency towards repetition and variation of individual phrases, particularly within longer melodic sections, for example, in the *bayt* of *barwal* 1, the *xafīf* and the *xatam*, and in the *ṭāla*^{c} of the *draj*. Further repetition is provided by instrumental responses and occasionally, vocal repetitions of individual phrases, as in the *xatam*.

The lengths of the melodic sections and their relative lengths within songs are variable. Thus, for example, in the first *barwal*, the *bayt* and *rujū*^{c} comprise twenty-one measures and the *ṭāla*^{c} ten. In the second *barwal*, all three sections are four measures in length. In the *bṭāyḥī*, the *bayt* and *rujū*^{c} comprise six measures and the *ṭāla*^{c} eight.

There tends to be little if any internal contrast of ^{c}*uqūd*: despite its name, signifying departure, the *ṭāla*^{c} does not necessarily introduce either new melodic material or a change in register. Such change as does occur generally involves a shift in tonal emphasis rather than the introduction of a new tonal area. The *ṭālaᶜ* of the *bṭāyḥī*, for example, opens with a contrasting melody reinforcing the lower register c-g and continues with a truncated version of the melody of the *bayt*. The *ṭālaᶜ* of the *draj* likewise restates melodic material from the *bayt*, focusing on the lower register, while the *ṭālaᶜ* of the *xafīf* is based entirely on melodic material from the *bayt*. The *ṭālaᶜ* of the *xatam*, omitted from el-Mahdi's performance but included in his transcription, is basically an expanded version of mm 21–24 of the *bayt*.

More decisive melodic departures occur in the *brāwil*. In the first *barwal*, the *ṭālaᶜ* introduces a new melody in the higher register, contrasting the predominantly lower register of the *bayt*; in the second *barwal*, the new melody introduces a new register with the introduction of *ᶜiqd* (-I).

Unlike the other instrumental interludes, which are not specifically related to any one piece, those of the *abyāt* anticipate the *ᶜuqūd* and, in the case of the *dxūl al-abyāt* and *fāriġa* 1, the melodic contour of the following vocal sections. Each instrumental and vocal pair focuses on a distinctive phase in an overall rising progression.

dxūl	c–g	(-I) (I)
bayt 1, first melody		
fāriġa 1	f/g–c	(II)
bayt 1, second melody		
fāriġa 2	c–g	(-I) (I)
bayt 2	c′–g′	(-I′) (I′)

The pattern is interrupted at the end of each vocal and instrumental section by a cadential descent to the final.

Tempo Fluctuation

The effect of continuous motion produced by the cyclic patterns of the *iqāᶜāt* is interrupted at the boundaries between the different *iqāᶜāt,* and it is nuanced by characteristic tempo fluctuations within certain songs, or groups of songs. In the *abyāt* (in el-Mahdi's and Zghonda's performances) the verses maintain a steady tempo in *iqāᶜ al-bṭāyḥī* until the end of the second *bayt,* where a sudden increase in tempo produces a seamless transition into the *barwal* section of the following *dxūl al-bṭāyḥiyya.* In all three performances, there is a gradual accelerando through the *brāwil.* This pattern is broken in the *draj* (in el-Mahdi's and Zghonda's performances) where there is a sudden increase in tempo in the *ṭālaᶜ*, a return to the previous speed in the *rujūᶜ*, and a final drop in speed at the last phrase.

THE *NŪBA* AND THE ARAB GARDEN

Snoussi's description of the Arab garden as a metaphor for the *nūba* illuminates qualities beyond the purely structural. In his garden, nature is cultivated for its aesthetic effect, as demonstrated in the view from the pavilion. Likewise the *nūba* is appreciated for its aesthetic qualities: unlike other forms of Tunisian entertainment music, typically associated with dancing, the *nūba* is music for listening: the audience, like the spectator in the pavilion, is still. The aesthetic function of the *nūba* is implicit in the term *mūsīqā fann* (literally, art music) used by some Tunisian intellectuals as an alternative designation for the *maᵓlūf.*

The *nūba* is associated with nature in its cyclic formal principles, in the natural imagery pervading its texts, and in the theoretical tradition that links the individual *nūbāt* with certain natural and temporal properties, including hours of the day. These properties were represented systematically in a symbolic "tree" of temperaments (*šajarat al-ṭubūᶜ*; Guettat 2000: 137). Like the plants and flowers of the garden, the melodies of the *maᵓlūf* are anonymous and impersonal, timeless and essentially unchanging, each performance a unique rendering of an undisclosed archetype.

The garden is a product of a long and continuing process of cultivation, nurture, and care. The *maᵓlūf* owes its survival through centuries of oral transmission, only latterly supported by notation, to the continuous patronage of individuals and institutions devoted to its preservation.

An Arab garden such as Snoussi describes is a privilege of the leisured classes, combining sensuous and aesthetic pleasures with ideals of refinement, taste, and conoisseurship. The *maᵓlūf* embodies similar values and ideals both in its melodic and poetic content and—in as much as it was traditionally cultivated by the aristocracy and urban elite—in its more rarified performance contexts. D'Erlanger's account of a *maʾlūf* concert in an aristocratic home (p. 56) opens with a description of the garden:

> Let us now make our way into the palace of a nobleman, even that of the prince. Courtyard follows upon courtyard, garden upon garden, one could get lost in such a maze: here an orange grove is surrounded by colonnades; there a pool reflects the high walls of this gigantic home, creating the illusion of an enchanted city . . .
>
> (D'Erlanger 1917:94).

Just as Snoussi's garden occupies a definite space, separated from its environment, so the *nūba* embraces a specific tonal space and repertory, and its performance is a circumscribed event whose various stages are marked by the fixed sequence of *iqāʿāt*. The circular wall surrounding the garden mirrors the cyclic principles of the *nūba* operating on various levels simultaneously: in the overall cycle of the thirteen *nūbāt*, the internal cycle of genres, and in the melodic and rhythmic-metric cycles of the individual pieces.

In Snoussi's garden, all the paths lead directly towards the center; in the *nūba*, the melodic lines gravitate towards the final, or tonal center which, like the observer's viewpoint, is constant throughout. No matter which way the observer turns, his view remains the same, undisturbed by any irregularity. The *nūba* is likewise tonally static, operating within a predetermined tonal area, colored in the present example by subtle shifts between *sīka* and *rāst* and the various transformations of *ʿiqd* (II). Between cadences on the final, phrases focus on the degrees framing the successive *ʿuqūd*, namely, c, e𝄳, g, and c'. The melodic patterning is similarly confined: typically stepwise, meandering, constantly treading back on itself, based on sequences, inversions, and other forms of repetition. The dynamic level is constant throughout.

The static quality extends to the unfolding of the performance as a whole. In *maqām* traditions, such as the Iranian *dastgah* or Iraqi *maqām*, whose sequencing principles are tonal-melodic, the overall melodic structure is typically progressive: tension increases as the successive tonal centers move consistently further from the final, reaching a climax at the point of maximum distance, and resolving with a cadential return to the final.

No comparable process occurs in the sequencing principles of the *nūba*: except for the accelerando characterising individual pieces, contrasts such as slow/fast, long/short, metered/unmetered, duple/triple, precomposed/improvised, vocal/instrumental, and solo/ensemble are juxtaposed in alternating rather than progressive sequences.

The melodic flow is continuous as the pieces follow one another without pause, the periodic shifts in tempi and from one rhythmic-metric cycle to the next comparable to changes in gear as a train passes through an unchanging landscape: the images along the way may vary in density and detail but the view, like that from the pavilion, stays essentially the same.

NOTES

1. Manoubi Snoussi was the personal secretary of the Baron Rodolphe d'Erlanger, author of the pioneering six-volume work *La Musique Arabe*, 1930–59 (see chapter 2). D'Erlanger acknowledged Snoussi's assistance in translating the Arab music theoretical texts of volumes 1–4 (D'Erlanger 1930: xvii–xviii). Snoussi was responsible for preparing the five posthumous volumes for publication, and he wrote the Preface to volume 6 outlining the major trends in Arab music since d'Erlanger's death in 1932 (D'Erlanger1959:vii–ix).

2. This popular view has been qualified by the Tunisian musicologist Mahmoud Guettat, who has argued that a similar type of music developed simultaneously in Islamic Spain and the Maghreb and that the Andalusian refugees merely enriched and reinforced a pre-existing tradition (2000: 215–16).

3. See Guettat 2000, 257 ff. for a comparative study of the four musical traditions.

4. In relation to other *maqām* traditions the *nūba* corresponds to the various Ottoman cyclic formats, or "suite" traditions, such as the Turkish *fasil*, the Mevlevi *ayin*, and the eastern Mediterranean *waṣla*, whose fundamental principle of sequencing is rhythmic-metric, rather than to those such as the Iraqi *maqām*, the Persian *dastgah,* or the Azeri *mugam-dastgah* whose sequencing principles are essentially tonal-melodic. See Davis 2001 for further discussion of these and other *maqām* concepts.

5. In Tunisia, the Arabic term "*šarqiyya*" (literally, "eastern") and the French "*orientale*" are used to distinguish the music of Egypt and the surrounding Levant from that of Tunisia (*musiqa tūnisiyya* or *musique tunisienne*). In this work, I use the term "Middle Eastern" in the sense corresponding to the Tunisian terms "*šarqiyya*" and "*orientale.*"

6. The institute was named after the aristocratic patron and amateur of the *maʾlūf* Muḥammad al-Rašid Bey (d. 1759).

7. Much of the published repertory, including the songs of the thirteen *nūbāt*, is reproduced in Boudhina 1992 (texts) and Boudhina 1995 (music).

8. In both el-Mahdi's and Fethi Zghonda's recordings of *nūbat al-sīka* (pp.

16–17), the *draj*, which opens the section in triple meter, has a slightly faster metronomic value than the preceding *barwal*, resulting in a steady increase in tempo throughout the performance. However, factors such as the length, density, and accentuation of the rhythmic cycle apparently override metronome values in determining the perceived speed: the *draj*, with its long, regular cycle and its heavy initial accentuation, feels slow, while the preceding *barwal*, with its short, relatively active, syncopated pattern, feels fast. In the notes to his recording of *nūbat al-sīka* Zghonda observes that "what is of particular note is its general structure in which slow and fast movements alternate in accordance with the conventional pattern of Tunisian *nūba*" (Zghonda 1994: 15).

9. In the published canon, only five *nūbāt* are provided with a *tūšiya* (see Table A, below). New *tawāšī*, commissioned by the Rashidiyya, have been composed for the remaining *nūbāt.*

10. In the *mṣaddar* of *nūbat al-sīka*, for example, the four *xānāt* comprise 4, 4, 4, and 5, measures respectively.

11. The *draj* and *xafīf* sections are preceded by brief instrumental introductions called *fāriġāt al-adrāj* and *fāriġāt al-xafāyif;* these are in the same *iqāᶜāt* as the songs which follow.

12. An *istaxbār* is a solo instrumental improvisation in free rhythm and the Tunisian equivalent of the Middle Eastern *taqsīm.*

13. This and other studies by el-Mahdi represent the modern Tunisian *maqām* theory taught in the state music educational establishments. The Tunisian musicologists Mahmoud Guettat and Mourad Shakli base their presentations of the Tunisian *maqāmāt* on el-Mahdi's study (Guettat 2000: 367–68; Shakli 1994: 116–131).

14. Marcus' scale is reproduced in Davis 2001: 832.

15. Following el-Mahdi, Mahmoud Guettat uses the same symbols in his presentation of the Tunisian *maqāmāt* (Guettat 2000: 367–68).

16. D'Erlanger attributes the *taqāsim* to the Syrian Shaykh ᶜAlī al-Darwīš and the *istaxbārāt* to the Tunisian Shaykh Khemais Tarnane.

17. In the 1970s, the Tunisian state record company, Ennaghem, reproduced various *nūbāt* recorded by the radio ensemble in the early 1960s.

18. *Nūbat al-ḏīl* (1959) and *nūbat al-ramal* (1960) were released in 1992, and *nūbat al-ᶜirāq* (1960) and *nūbat al-aṣbahān* (1962) were released in 1993.

19. Bushnak interprets el-Mahdi's first *barwal* as a *dxūl barwal* and el-Mahdi's *draj* as a *barwal.*

20. Example 4c is derived from Zghonda's description of *maqām al-sīka* in the notes to his recording. The scale illustrating his notes does not contain all the accidentals he describes. However, Zghonda explained to me that the scale is printed incorrectly.

Chapter Two

The Baron Rodolphe d'Erlanger

From 1921 until his death in 1932, the baron Rodolphe d'Erlanger established himself in his newly completed palace in Sidi Bou Said, a clifftop village on the outskirts of Tunis, and dedicated himself to the revival and conservation of traditional Tunisian music.

He was born on 7 June, 1872, in Boulogne sur Seine, France, the third and youngest son of a wealthy banker of German Jewish extraction and an American heiress.[1] Rather than follow his brothers into the family bank, Rodolphe studied art at the Académie Julian in Paris, and he subsequently followed a lifelong career as a painter specializing in landscapes, portraits, and local scenes on oil and canvas, inspired by his travels in North Africa.

In 1911, d'Erlanger settled with his American wife Bettina and their son Leo in Tunisia, where he had inherited substantial lands and property. They were attracted to Sidi Bou Said by its natural beauty and its mild coastal climate, which d'Erlanger believed would benefit his fragile health. Over the following decade, he supervised the construction, by artisans from across the Maghreb, of his magnificent Moorish palace, Ennajma Ezzahra (resplendent star), on the cliffs of Sidi Bou Said, overlooking the sea.

D'Erlanger's initiation into Arab music dates from 1914, when he first encountered the Tunisian musician and scholar Shaykh Ahmed el-Wafi (1850–1921). El-Wafi was born in the medina of Tunis to a prosperous, erudite family of Andalusian descent; he was an unrivalled master of the *maʾlūf*, equally knowledgable in *qurʾanic* recitation, Sufi repertories, and eastern Arab styles. He became d'Erlanger's personal mentor and friend in an intensive collaboration which continued to the end of the shaykh's life.

D'Erlanger outlined his musical ideology and his vision for the *maʾlūf* in an article entitled "Au sujet de la musique arabe en Tunisie," published in Tunis in 1917. The article begins with a description of traditional social contexts for the *maʾlūf*. These included the *zawāya* (s. *zāwiya*), or Sufi meeting places, which effectively served as music clubs and conservatories where pupils of all social classes could learn "the entire art music tradition" under the tutelage of a shaykh; celebrations for religious and family festivals such as weddings and circumcisions; amateur music making in the idyllic gardens and luxurious chambers of aristocratic homes; and cafés, where professional musicians gathered to rehearse (D'Erlanger 1917:93).[2]

In the *zawāya*, Sufi musicians rehearsed the *maʾlūf* alongside their sacred repertories, both for recreation and entertainment and as an act of duty to conserve the Andalusian heritage. The *maʾlūf* was typically sung after the weekly *ḥaḍrāt* (Sufi religious ceremonies; s. *ḥaḍra*), which were open to the community at large. The ceremonies included special chants, breathing techniques and bodily movements whose function was to induce trance; the *maʾlūf* was supposed to calm the heightened emotional atmosphere and the performances also provided opportunities to learn the repertory since everyone present joined in the singing. The profane texts (*kalām al-hazl*) were sometimes substituted by religious ones (*kalām al-jadd*), or they were retained and interpreted allegorically, as "images of paradise."

The *zawāya* also functioned as springboards for music making in secular contexts. In many towns, Sufi musicians sang *maʾlūf xam* in the local cafés, in street processions and pilgrimages, and in family and communal celebrations. Elsewhere, in the beylical palaces and in certain towns, notably Tunis, the *maʾlūf* was performed outside the *zawāya* by small ensembles of solo vocalists and instrumentalists, including melody instruments (p. 7).

Legendary among such ensembles was that led by the *ʿūd ʿarbī* player Shaykh Khemais Tarnane at the Café M'rabbet in the medina of Tunis. Every Friday morning through the late 1920s and early 1930s, the ensemble performed a complete *nūba*, following the conventional cycle of *nūbāt*, to a large, dedicated following. Recalling these sessions, which he had attended as a child, the *rabāb* player Dr. Belhassan Farza described them to me as a veritable "school for the *maʾlūf*."

Hamadi Bougamha, *naqqārāt* player in the *ma'lūf* ensemble of Sidi Bou Said, showed me a picture hanging on a wall in his living room of the ensemble that performed in the *Café des Nattes* in the early 1950s.[3] Hamadi assured me that the picture was true to life; he was in it himself as a young man, singing. It depicted seven musicians, including the shaykh on the *ṭār*, a *naqqārāt* player, Hamadi, and two additional singers; they were joined by two musicians from Tunis playing mandolin and *nāy*. The musicians were dressed in the traditional Tunisian *jabāyib* (s. *jibba*: long wide-sleeved coat), and they were seated on wooden chairs or cross legged on mats around a large oblong stone slab laid with tiny cups of coffee and plates of dried dates stuffed with butter. Two men sat at a small wooden table to one side, rolling *taqruri* (hashish); the dates were supposed to counteract the effects of lowered blood sugar produced by the hashish. Sometimes a *darbūka* joined the ensemble but its tone was too harsh for the *taqruri* smokers who usually forced it to stop.

In his article, d'Erlanger gives a vivid account of a *ma'lūf* concert in an aristocratic home:

> Let us now make our way into the palace of a nobleman, or even that of the Prince. Courtyard succeeds courtyard, garden succeeds garden, one could get lost in such a maze: here, an orange grove is surrounded by colonnades, there, a pool reflects the high walls of this gigantic residence giving the impression of being in an enchanted city. The master of the house . . . is looking forward to the night, when he will gather his close friends around him and summon his musicians. He too will take part in the concert; he may play the lute or, if he is gifted with a melodious voice, he will sing . . . he will take great care to prevent any discordant element from marring the listeners' appreciation. He will have chosen the finest room in his palace for his concert hall; his musicians will be wearing the most magnificent costumes, and everyone around him will be dressed in harmonious colors. No sound will be allowed to distract the listeners; the servants who wait on him will be shod in the softest leather. The low tables will be laden with the most beautiful dishes containing savories and sweetmeats; perfumes will drift through the atmosphere; often in his rapture he will forget the passing hours . . .
>
> (1917: 94)

D'Erlanger then contrasts the rich musical past with its current state of decadence:

> Bars and nightclubs have displaced the *zawāya*. There are no more street processions and fewer people go on pilgrimages. The musicians have forsaken the cafés, and one hears there only the hoarse coughing of the hashish smokers as their cards slap rhythmically onto the tables. The prince has abandoned his private ensemble to listen to a brass band in which foreign instruments vainly blast out notes that grate on the ears. The palaces are crumbling, and their music is dying.
>
> (1917: 94)

He attached particular blame for the corruption of Tunisian music on the beys (Turkish rulers) for inviting to their courts European music teachers to instruct their musicians. In their ignorance of the principles of Arab music the Europeans had created "an illegitimate type of music which has neither rational basis, nor aesthetic appeal" (1917: 95). In his introduction to the fifth volume of *La Musique Arabe,* d'Erlanger laments the widespread use of European instruments of fixed pitch such as the piano, harmonium, and the fretted mandolin whose tunings are incompatible with the variable, non-temperered intervals of the *maqāmāt* (1949: 341).

Ultimately, however, d'Erlanger believed that the roots of decadence were inherent in the musical culture itself. Transmitted orally through the centuries, without theoretical support, this music had depended for its survival on musicians who were increasingly ignorant of its rules, and whose sole concern was to conserve, rather than develop, whatever vestiges of the tradition remained (1949: 337–338; 340–341). "The Arab musicians of North Africa offer no more than a passive resistance to the decadence of their art, which is dying slowly but surely, contenting themselves merely with transmitting, albeit with laudable zeal, an increasingly declining repertory which each day suffers further losses" (1949: 341).

D'Erlanger concluded his article of 1917 with a proposal for the revival of the *maʾlūf*. He insisted that Europeans should on no account attempt to teach Arab musicians themselves; rather they should limit their contribution to supporting the efforts of native musicians. In particular, d'Erlanger encouraged European scholars to provide Arab musicians with a theoretical basis for their teaching. "We sincerely hope that one day we shall be given the opportunity to provide the shaykhs of Arab music with the means of explaining to their pupils all the rules of that art" (1917: 95).

D'Erlanger dedicated the rest of his life to achieving that goal. He gathered together an entourage of outstanding Tunisian musicians and scholars and turned his palace into a center of Arab musical performance and scholarship. Believing that in order to construct a modern music theory, it was necessary to know the theoretical traditions of the past, his first priority was to rediscover those traditions and make them accessible to European scholars. To this end, d'Erlanger supervised the translation into French of major Arab treatises on music dating from the tenth to the sixteenth centuries including writings by al-Fārābī, ibn Sīnā (Avicenne), Ṣafī al-dīn, and al-Lāḏiqī. The main fruits of this activity, presented in the first four volumes of *La Musique Arabe*, are summarized below:

Vol 1 (1930) al-Fārābī's *Kitāb al-Mūsīqī al-Kabīr*, books 1 and 2.
Vol 2 (1935) al-Fārābī's *Kitāb al-Mūsīqī al-Kabīr,* book 3; a small treatise of ibn Sīnā (Avicenne) (Mathematics, ch. 12) extracted from *Kitāb al-Šifā*ᵓ.
Vol 3 (1938) The first complete translation of Ṣafī al-dīn's monumental two-part work: *al-Risālat al-Šarafiyya* and *Kitāb al-Adwār* (book of musical cycles).
Vol 4 (1939) Anonymous treatise dedicated to Ottoman Sultan Muḥammad II (1451–1481) comprising a compilation of al-Fārābī, ibn Sīnā, and Ṣafī al-dīn; al-Lāḏiqī's *Risālat al-Fatḥiyyah*.

THE 1932 CAIRO CONGRESS AND ITS PROJECTS

It was d'Erlanger's role as both co-organizer and contributor to the First International Congress of Arab Music, held in Cairo in 1932, that enabled him to bring his project to completion. Sponsored by King Fuᵓād and supported by the Egyptian government, the Congress was intended to provide an international forum in which eminent European musicians and scholars would collaborate with their Egyptian and other Middle Eastern colleagues to discuss "all that was required to make the music civilised, and to teach it and rebuild it on acknowledged scientific principles" (*Kitāb* 1933: 19).[4]

D'Erlanger's contribution to the Congress involved the preparation of a comprehensive classification of the melodic modes and rhythmic forms of Arab music in current use. At his request, the Egyptian government sent the Syrian Shaykh ᶜAlī al-Darwīš to Sidi Bou Said to assist him in his task (1949: 381). The results of their collaboration were published in both the Arabic (1933) and the French (1934) Congress proceedings and, in an expanded version, they constitute volumes 5 (on the general scale and melodic modes) and 6 (on the rhythms and compositional forms) of *La Musique Arabe*.

In the introduction to *La Musique Arabe 5,* d'Erlanger acknowledges three further sources for his study. These were the Tunisian Shaykhs Ahmed el-Wafi and Khemais Tarnane, who provided the modes and rhythms of the Arab Andalusian tradition, and the Lebanese Christian scholar Professor Iskandar Šalfūn, director of a private music conservatory in Cairo[5] (1949: xiii–xiv). D'Erlanger specifically acknowledged "the methodological spirit" of Professor Šalfūn who was "initiated into the analytical procedures of the ancient Arab theorists" (1949: xvi).

D'Erlanger's reports for the Cairo Congress are a landmark in the history of Arab music theory. Introducing his presentation he writes "this is the first time that the Arab modes . . . have been analysed and broken down into genres. This work will have a fundamental importance for later studies which will have an aim of establishing a scientific theory of Arab music on a solid base" (1934: 136, quoted in Marcus 1989: 278). In his introduction to *La Musique Arabe* 5 he claims to "introduce for the first time, in the study of modern Arab music, the analytical methods preconceived by the ancient Arab theorists. . . ." (1949: viii). In effect, d'Erlanger reintroduced into mainstream Arab music theory the medieval concept of the tetrachord, or "genre" (Arabic *jins*, pl. *ajnās*; from the Greek genus) as the fundamental modal unit.

The concept of tetrachords had been reintroduced into modern Turkish music theory earlier in the twentieth century by Rauf Yekta Bey (Yekta Bey: 1922). Shaykh ᶜAlī al-Darwiš, who had graduated from the Turkish Music Institute, Dār al-Alḥan, in Istanbul, would doubtless have been familiar with this analytical method (Marcus 1989: 671–2; 709); d'Erlanger himself, moreover, would have encountered the concept of *jins* in his extensive studies of medieval Arab music theory. However, in *La Musique Arabe*, d'Erlanger attributes both the application of tetrachordal theory and the use of the term *ᶜiqd* (pl. *ᶜuqūd*; literally, necklace) to his Lebanese informant Professor Iskandar Šalfūn.

> In order to describe the scales and the modal combinations the Professor Iskandar Shalfoun analysed them in small groups of homogenous notes, this is to say, in genres, but in order to designate these small melodic series, he employed, for the first time in Arabic music literature, the term *ᶜiqd* (pl. *ᶜuqūd*) which means "necklace."
>
> (d'Erlanger 1949: 71).

D'Erlanger's Arabic language report was particularly influential among contemporary Arab music theorists and the concept of the tetrachord has remained a fundamental principle of modern *maqām* theory (Marcus 1989: 48–49). In Tunisia, Salah el-Mahdi claims to have consulted d'Erlanger's examples in both the Cairo Congress proceedings and in *La Musique Arabe* for his presentation of the Tunisian *maqāmāt* (*al-Turāṯ* 8:18). However, it was through the activities of his informant, Shaykh ᶜAlī al-Darwīš, rather than through either of his publications, that d'Erlanger's work had its greatest impact on Tunisian musicians generally.

In 1931, during Shaykh ᶜAlī 's visit to Sidi Bou Said, d'Erlanger arranged for him to give public classes in Arab music theory in the medina of Tunis, funded by the Tunisian government. In these classes, the Syrian musician introduced his Tunisian students to modern Arab music theory, applying for the first time the concept of *ᶜuqūd* to the Tunisian *maqāmāt* (1949: 381). Such was the success of these classes that, in 1938, the members of the recently founded Rashidiyya ensemble invited Shaykh ᶜAlī to return to Tunis as their mentor. During this second visit, Shaykh ᶜAlī effectively established the teaching methods and syllabus of the Rashidiyya school. These in turn became the foundation for the curriculum of the state music conservatories after Tunisian independence in 1956 (el-Mahdi 1981: 68).

D'Erlanger was too ill to attend the Congress (he died in October that year) and his reports were presented in his absence by Shaykh ᶜAlī al-Darwīš. The Shaykh also escorted to Cairo d'Erlanger's *maᵓlūf* ensemble. This comprised Mohamed Ghanem on the *rabāb*, Khemais Tarnane on the *ᶜūd ᶜarbī*, Khemais el-Ati on the *naqqārāt*, Ali ibn Arafa on the *ṭār*, and the solo, falsetto vocalist Mohamed ibn Hasan (el-Mahdi 1981: 27; Moussali 1988: 146).

In Cairo, the Tunisian musicians performed alongside groups from Morocco, Algeria, Egypt, Syria, Lebanon, and Iraq, and they participated in recording sessions directed by Robert Lachmann, assisted by Béla Bartók. The recordings, produced on 78-rpm disks by His Master's Voice, England, provide unique documentation of an archaic type of performance practice that was soon to become obsolete with the dissolution of d'Erlanger's ensemble after his death.[6]

On their return to Tunis the musicians reported the recommendation of the Congress that institutions be established throughout the Arab world for the conservation and promotion of traditional Arab music. Tunisians acknowledge that this recommendation served as a catalyst for the founding of the Rashidiyya Institute in Tunis, just two years later (el-Mahdi 1981: 27–8).

* * *

On 29 October, 1932, d'Erlanger died from bronchial disease, aged sixty. He was buried beneath the vault of a small white mausoleum, enclosed by trees, in the garden of Ennajma Ezzahra. Engraved in Arabic on his tombstone is the following anonymous poem written in the name of "ᶜāᵓilat al-mūsīqā al-tūnisiyya" (the family of Tunisian music).[7]

In 1987, d'Erlanger's ashes were transferred to the family home in Montreux, Switzerland, and the following year, Ennajma Ezzahra was handed over to the Tunisian government. On 20 December 1991, the Centre des Musiques Arabes et Méditerranéennes was inaugurated there under the auspices of the Ministry of Culture. The CMAM houses the Tunisian national sound archive and a museum devoted to d'Erlanger's life and work. Its activities include research projects, exhibitions, conferences, and concerts.

EPILOGUE

Situated on a hill some twenty kilometers north-east of Tunis, just north of Carthage, the village of Sidi Bou Said was traditionally a center for the *maᵓlūf*. Since the eighteenth century the Tunisian aristocracy had built their palaces there. The village was famous for its *zawāya*, its *xarjāt* (Sufi processions), and the cafés and pilgrims' hospices that were attached to the *zawāya*. The cafés attracted musicians from Tunis who brought their instruments and performed the *maᵓlūf* with the local Sufi *firqa*. D'Erlanger's descriptions (1917: 92–94) of the aristocrat passing his nights in the luxurious atmosphere of his private concert, the *firqa* practising under the shaykh of the *zāwiya*, the musicians playing in the idyllic gardens and jasmine scented rooms of the villas, and the women crowding to listen to them behind the grilles that separated them from the men, were traditional scenes for the *maᵓlūf* in Sidi Bou Said; and the aristocrat was d'Erlanger himself.

When I first visited Sidi Bou Said in the early 1980s, older residents recalled the baron perambulating the streets of the village, carrying his

In recognition of your deeds

A testimony of your golden contributions to literature and the Arts
a tear is shed for you by the music of the Arabs
which, with your cultivation, became eternal and adorned the best of times.
O baron, if your eminent presence has closed its eyes to the world and
become veiled it is our duty to remember that
which is due to you, which will not be forgotten.
And this is a testimony of loyalty which the Arts depict for their father.

1932 The Family of Tunisian Music 1351

ᶜūd, singing the *maᵓlūf*. D'Erlanger also patronized the local *zawāya*. An elderly Sufi sat with me on the rugs on the floor of the *zāwiya* of the ᶜĪsāwiyya and described how the baron had learned the *maᵓlūf* in the same place. D'Erlanger asked two musicians to repeat the same phrase, then he chose the version he considered the more beautiful and requested the other musician to learn it too. This memory provides a precedent for Mohamed Triki's method of producing a standard version of the *maᵓlūf* for the Rashidiyya.

While the European colonizers are generally remembered for their ignorance and contempt of indigenous cultural traditions, Tunisians acknowledge d'Erlanger's pivotal role in promoting those traditions and acquiring for them renewed dignity and respect. Through his connections with musicians, scholars and patrons in other Arab countries, the production of *La Musique Arabe* and his central role in the Cairo Congress, d'Erlanger ensured that the Tunisians' efforts on behalf of the *maᵓlūf* were realized within an international context for the modernization of traditional Arab music.

NOTES

1. His father was the baron Frédéric Émile d'Erlanger and his mother, Marguerite Mathilde d'Erlanger (née Slidell). Rodolphe was raised in the Catholic faith.

2. The society d'Erlanger depicts is almost exclusively male; the only reference to women occurs in *maᵓlūf* concert in a private home where they strain to listen "concealed behind grilles."

3. Occupying a prime position at the highest point of the village, overlooking the souk, the *Café des Nattes* is attached to the marabout of the patron saint Abu Said. In the eighteenth century, the main entrance was converted into the entrance of the café and the side entrance, previously reserved for women, became the common entrance to the marabout (Zbiss 1971: 36).

4. See Racy 1987 for a detailed account of the 1932 Cairo Congress and Davis 1993 for details of the Tunisian contribution.

5. Salfūn was also the editor of the first Arab music journal, *Rawḍat al-Balābil* (The Garden of Nightingales). Cairo, 1920-28. D'Erlanger provides biographical notes for his informants in 1949: 378–84.

6. Examples of the Tunisian recordings are included on AAA 094: 1984 and APN 88-10: 1988.

7. The Arabic poem is taken from Louati 1995:48. The translation is by Kathryn Stapley, The Oriental Institute, Oxford.

Chapter Three

The Rashidiyya Ensemble: From Oral to Written Tradition

In November 1934, the Rashidiyya Institute was founded in Tunis with the aim of conserving and promoting traditional Tunisian music and encouraging new Tunisian composition.[1] It was named after the eighteenth century aristocratic patron and amateur of the *maʾlūf,* Muḥammad al-Rašīd Bey (d. 1759). The seventy-one founders included professional and amateur musicians, writers, poets, doctors, lawyers, administrators, and politicians, and their elected president was Mustapha Sfar, mayor of Tunis. As the first public secular organization devoted to Tunisian music, the Rashidiyya provided the indigenous counterpart to the French music conservatory, founded in Tunis in 1896. It was granted the official status of an *"Association"* and it was subsidized by the government of the Protectorate.[2]

In pursuit of its goals, the Rashidiyya created a new, enlarged type of ensemble inspired by Western and contemporary Egyptian ensembles; it established systematic teaching based on solfège and Western notation and, in an attempt to standardize the diverse interpretations of its musicians, it transcribed the entire repertory of the *maʾlūf* from oral tradition into Western staff notation for use in teaching and performance.[3] Rather than crystallise the melodies into one standard version, however, the original transcriptions provided the impetus for successive layers of prescriptive notations, each reflecting the individual preferences of subsequent leaders of the ensemble. After Tunisian independence in 1956, the Ministry of Cultural Affairs published the Rashidiyya's transcriptions in a series of nine volumes, edited by Salah el-Mahdi, entitled *al-Turāṯ al-Mūsīqī al-Tūnīsī/Patrimoine Musical Tunisien (The Tunisian*

Musical Heritage). Distributed to newly created educational and recreational institutions throughout the country, the published notations became the basis of a new national performing tradition inspired by the Rashidiyya.[4]

In this chapter I consider the background and circumstances in which Western notation was adopted by the Rashidiyya and I compare the contrasting ideologies and methods underlying its use by successive leaders of the ensemble.

******

Western staff notation had been used in teaching and performing the *maʾlūf* nearly a century before the founding of the Rashidiyya, in the specialized sphere of the military band. In 1840, Ahmed Bey I established a Western-style military academy to train army officers and, to complete his project, he invited European music teachers to create a band. The Europeans introduced the Tunisian musicians to Western wind instruments, staff notation and a staple repertory of diatonic fanfares. In addition, the beylical band performed melodies from the *maʾlūf* transcribed into Western notation.[5]

Civilian wind bands, modelled on their French counterparts, arose in the early twentieth century. They performed a similar repertory to the beylical band, including the *maʾlūf*, in street processions and in public and domestic festivities such as weddings. The largest band, *al-jamᶜiyya al-Nasiriyya* (f. 1905) hosted classes in solmization and notation led by d'Erlanger's mentor Shaykh Ahmed el-Wafi (Guettat 2000: 237).

The story of how notation was adopted by the Rashidiyya was explained to me in dramatic detail by the original leader of the ensemble, Mohamed Triki. In their efforts to conserve and promote the *maʾlūf* the founders of the Rashidiyya invited the most outstanding shaykhs of Tunis to form an ensemble. The initial response produced six violins, two *rabābāt* (s. *rabāb*), five *aᶜwād* (s. ᶜūd), three *qawānīn* (s. *qānūn*), *ṭār*, *naqqārāt*, six male vocalists, and one female singer [6] (el-Mahdi 1981: 49–50).

Such an ensemble was unprecedented both in its size and in the variety and combination of its instruments. The crucial difference, however, was that it combined several instruments of the same type. As a result, heterophony was replaced by cacophony. Triki described to me the chaos of the early rehearsals, the shaykhs all vying with one another as to whose interpretation was the best. Evidently the musicians needed to agree on a standard version of the melodies, and the Rashidiyya's leadership decided that this could best be achieved through the use of notation, in emulation of Western practice. At this point the young violinist Mohamed Triki, versatile in Western, Middle Eastern and Tunisian music, was invited to supervise the transcription of the entire repertory, teach the musicians how to read the notations and lead them in performance.[7]

Triki revelled in recounting to me how the president of the Rashidiyya and mayor of Tunis, Mustafa Sfar, begged him to join the ensemble in order to "save the Tunisian heritage." Triki described his very first working session with the shaykhs when Sfar assembled the musicians and introduced them to their new leader. Sfar had hit upon a strategy that would facilitate the old men's acceptance of the young man's direction: Triki would pose as their student. Triki selected an instrumental piece, the *mṣaddar* of *nūbat al-aṣbahān* and requested each shaykh to play it phrase by phrase in turn. After they had all performed the first phrase Triki asked them to consult with one another and agree on the best version, which he then transcribed. Triki took his "teachers" through the whole piece in this way, notating each phrase as it was chosen. Finally he played them the complete transcription. The result, a composite of various parts of several different interpretations of the same piece was unfamiliar to everyone; nevertheless, each shaykh recognised the portions he had contributed and everyone had to admit that this was the version they had agreed upon.

Once the shaykhs had accepted Triki's project he relaxed his methods and most of the transcriptions are based on performances by one or two sources only. Chief among these was Shaykh Khemais Tarnane, d'Erlanger's former mentor and the original leader of the Rashidiyya chorus.[8] Not all the sources, however, were members of the Rashidiyya: Triki described to me how he and his colleagues knocked at the doors of musicians throughout the city in their attempts to track down informants who, for a fee, could be persuaded to impart the rare repertory they had stored in their memories.

Finally, fair copies of the transcriptions were stored in the Rashidiyya's archives, eventually to become sources for the notations in *al-Turāṯ al-mūsīqī al-Tūnīsī* (el-Mahdi n.d.:12). Triki emphasized, however, that the primary purpose of the transcriptions was to provide standard versions for performance; they were never conceived as a means of preservation in themselves. I found a unanimous agreement among musicians that the transcriptions could never function as independent sources of the melodies: they were *aides-mémoires* and as such, they facilitated learning, but all insisted that it would be impossible to learn new pieces from notation alone.

During the first decade of his leadership Triki created a standard format for the ensemble which he acknowledged was influenced by the sonorities of both the Western symphony orchestra and contemporary Egyptian ensembles; at the same time, he established conventions of rehearsing and performing which have survived until the present. The ensemble comprised a nucleus of Western bowed strings, in unison and octaves, colored by various traditional Arab melody instruments such as the *ᶜūd ᶜarbī, ᶜūd šarqī, qānūn, rabāb,* and *nāy,* and a percussion section of *darbūka, ṭār* and *naqqārāt*; to this was added a separate male and female chorus. The instrumental texture was dominated by the violins, synchronized, according to Triki, "like an army of soldiers."

Rehearsal and performance followed different patterns for the instrumental and vocal sections. Since the nuances of the vocal line were considered too subtle to be taught other than by direct imitation, the singers learned the repertory from the chorus master, Shaykh Khemais Tarnane, by the traditional method of repetition and memorization; the instrumentalists, in contrast, were coached by Triki, aided by parts hand copied from the original transcriptions. When both sections had mastered a piece they would reunite to rehearse and perform under Triki; the chorus from memory and the instrumentalists from notation. Triki himself either led the ensemble from within, playing the violin, or more characteristically, he directed it from the front with a baton, like the conductor of a Western orchestra.

The shaykhs resisted the efforts of first Triki, then various European musicians, to teach them the techniques of solmization and notation. Finally, in 1938, the Rashidiyya invited their original mentor, d'Erlanger's informant Shaykh ᶜAlī al-Darwīš, back from Egypt to take over the task. The Shaykh's results were positive, and the following year he returned to Egypt, considering the Tunisians equipped to manage on their own (el-Mahdi 1981: 67–8). During his visit Shaykh ᶜAlī established the basic curriculum of the Rashidiyya school; this comprised solmization, notation, theory of both the Tunisian and Middle Eastern *maqāmāt* and *iqāᶜāt*, Arab music history, and instrumental performance. By the late 1940s, the ensemble was restricting its new membership to graduates of its school.

ALTERNATIVE TRANSCRIPTIONS

Over the years, Triki's transcriptions were succeeded by other notated versions of the repertory prepared by subsequent leaders of the Rashidiyya and its offshoot, the radio *maʾlūf* ensemble. The first musician openly to espouse the ideology of preparing fresh notations and to admit to doing so in practice was Abdulhamid Belalgia, director of the Tunisian radio ensemble, established in 1958. Incorporating the élite of the Rashidiyya's past and present membership, the radio ensemble was modelled on contemporary Egyptian radio and film orchestras and it added to the basic format of the Rashidiyya various electronic and other non-Arab instruments. Within this framework, a special reduced ensemble was formed for the *maʾlūf*. This comprised a chorus of ten male and ten female singers led by Khemais Tarnane, ten violins, two cellos, a double bass, a *qānūn*, a *nāy*, an *ᶜūd ᶜarbī*, and a percussion section of *darbūka*, *ṭār*, and *naqqārāt*.[9]

Belalgia aimed to distinguish his professional radio musicians from the "amateurs" of the Rashidiyya by introducing new "professional' standards of performance; effectively, he applied to the *maʾlūf* the Western orchestral conventions that had been established in performances of popular media songs, or *aġānī*, since the 1940s (Shakli 1994: 219–221). In contrast to Triki's notations, which give a single undifferentiated melodic line for both vocal and instrumental renderings, Belalgia prepared separate parts for each type of instrument: in general, the cellos and basses articulate the *iqāᶜ*, reinforcing the percussion in a reduced version of the melody, while the remaining instruments play the complete melody with characteristic embellishments. His scores contrast effects of timbre and register between the various instruments and voices and between pizzicato and arco strings; they synchronize bowings and they include details of tempo, dynamics, and phrasing.

Belalgia transcribed his own versions of the melodies which, he maintained, differed in significant details from the Rashidiyya's notations. He defended the legitimacy of his versions on grounds of authenticity rather than originality, claiming that they were derived from his extensive experience of the *maʾlūf* traditions of the *zawāyā*. Just as in oral tradition, the shaykh would teach his personal version of the melodies to his ensemble, so, Belalgia maintained, it was appropriate for him, as leader in a written tradition, to notate his own version of the melodies.

Belalgia insisted that there was no such thing as a definitive version of the *maʾlūf.* In oral tradition, the melodies were constantly being recreated through improvisation; it followed therefore that corresponding changes should be incorporated into the written tradition by constantly revising the notations. Belalgia regarded each transcription he made as provisional, intended for a particular performance or series of performances, to be replaced by fresh transcriptions on subsequent occasions. In this way, he believed, his transcriptions would reflect the essentially improvisatory nature of the *maʾlūf* thereby legitimizing the exclusion of improvization from performance.

Evidently, however, this ideal proved too cumbersome to be realized in practice. From 1972 to 1979, and again in 1992, Belalgia was appointed leader of the Rashidiyya; on each occasion he replaced the existing musicians by members of the radio ensemble.[10] All those I interviewed, both in the early 1980s and in the mid-1990s, maintained that Belalgia had simply imported to the Rashidiyya his original scores for the radio ensemble. They conceded, however, that he sometimes scribbled in minor alterations.

In 1979, Mohamed Saada succeeded Belalgia as leader of the Rashidiyya. Espousing his predecessor's ideologies, Saada created his own notations which, he maintained, represented his personal interpretations of the melodies. Like Belalgia, he claimed that his versions were rooted in the traditions of the *zawāyā*. Saada prepared separate parts for each instrument, and he generally maintained the orchestral conventions established by Belalgia. Occasionally, however, he admitted to compromising his ideals and using Belalgia 's scores instead of preparing his own.

A radically opposing ideology regarding the status and function of the Rashidiyya's notations was propagated by Salah el-Mahdi who succeeded Triki as leader of the ensemble in 1949. Apart from a few short-lived interruptions, el-Mahdi held the reins until 1972, when he was replaced by Belalgia. During this period, el-Mahdi rose to become the leading political force in Tunisian music. In 1961, he was simultaneously appointed Director of Music and Popular Arts in the newly established Ministry of Culture and Director of the National Conservatory of Music, positions he held until 1979. In his capacity of Director of Music and Popular Arts, el-Mahdi was personally responsible for the musical policies adopted by the government. These included the publication and distribution of the nine volumes of *Al-Turāṯ al-mūsīqī al-tūnīsī* containing the Rashidiyya's transcriptions of the *maʾlūf.*

In our conversations, el-Mahdi described the published notations as "note-for-note reproductions" of Triki's original transcriptions, although he acknowledged making some slight modifications in order to simplify certain details of rhythm and phrasing. In his introduction to the third volume of *al-Turāṯ* and again, in his official history of the Rashidiyya Institute, el-Mahdi refers to three national congresses, at Tabarka, Tozeur, and Carthage, organized by the Ministry of Culture in the early 1960s, at which recordings were made of all the *nūbāt* known to shaykhs representing all the regions of Tunisia. The recordings were subsequently transcribed and compared by a literary committee headed by Mohamed Lahbib and a musical committee headed by Mohamed Triki. According to el-Mahdi, the results of the comparisons revealed "no fundamental differences" ("*farūq jawhariyya*") between the musical interpretations (n.d.a.:12; 1981: 81–82). Thus, as their title "The Tunisian Musical Heritage" implies, the published notations are presented as a unitary national tradition."[11]

Triki for his part denied in our conversations that the recordings of the shaykhs had been comprehensive or that any systematic transcriptions or comparisons had been made. I could not find anyone who would admit to having heard the recordings or seen the alleged transcriptions and el-Mahdi himself claimed that they were lost. In general, I found considerable controversy over the alleged homogeneity of the Tunisian *maᶜlūf* and the status of the published notations. Many establishment musicians, including representatives of the Rashidiyya, the National Conservatory, and the Ministry of Culture itself, held the view that there were in fact distinctive regional variants.

Evidently the purpose of the three congresses was to establish the authority of the notations published by the Ministry of Culture as a unitary national tradition. Intended for use in the newly established educational and recreational institutions throughout the country, they represented, according to el-Mahdi, the sole "correct" version of the melodies. He admitted that it was legitimate, indeed desirable, for talented, experienced musicians to improvize embellishments in solo performance (as indeed he himself would demonstrate); nevertheless, he insisted that the published notations comprised all the essential melodic details.

MUSICAL EVIDENCE FROM TUNIS

Musical example 6 compares el-Mahdi's, Belalgia's, and Saada's notations of the *abyāt* of *nūbat al-aṣbahān* with the original transcription by Mohamed Triki. *Nūbat al-aṣbahān* was the principal item rehearsed and performed by the Rashidiyya during the 1982–83 season; it was apparently the favorite *nūba* of Shaykh Khemais Tarnane and it was one of the most comprehensively recorded *nūbat* in the archive of the ERTT.[12] All four leaders approved my choice of the *abyāt* on the grounds that, as a serious genre with a relatively long, slow rhythmic cycle, it offered rich scope for embellishment and individual interpretation.

The *abyāt* (literally, verses; s. *bayt*) is the introductory vocal genre of the *nūba*. As described (p. 9), it comprises two verses of a poem in literary Arabic set to a melody in *iqā*ᶜ *bṭāyḥī*. The first *bayt* is repeated to a different melody, and the three vocal sections are separated by instrumental interludes called *fāriġāt*.

The four sources are designated R35, TMH, RE60, and R82 as follows:

R35 The original transcription made by Mohamed Triki in 1935.
TMH The published version (*al-Turāṯ* 8:50–51).
RE62 Master notations prepared by Abdulhamid Belalgia for a studio performance of *nūbat al-aṣbahān* by the radio *ma*ᵓ*lūf* ensemble recorded by the ERTT on 19.7.62.
R82 Master notations prepared by Mohamed Saada for a public performance of *nūbat al-aṣbahān* by the Rashidiyya ensemble, recorded by myself at the National Conservatory of Music on 5.11.82.[13]

Musical example 6 reproduces the vocal sections only. (The *fāriġāt* are virtually identical in each source.) The first *bayt* of the *abyāt* is set to mm. 1–10, and it is repeated to a different melodic setting in mm. 10–19. The second *bayt* is set to mm. 19–26 (mm. 19–28 in RE60 and R82).

In the published notations, the text is presented in Arabic script broken into syllables beneath the notes. In Example 6, the syllables are reproduced in transliteration beneath TMH. The complete Arabic text, taken from *al-Turāṯ 8*: 35, is given in transliteration and English translation following Example 6.

Example 7 presents the scales of *maqām al-aṣbahān* according to d'Erlanger (1949: 368) and el-Mahdi (n.d.b.: 33).

Example 8 presents the ᶜ*uqūd* used in each source. In the following discussion, the *'uqud* are designated I, II, and III (as shown in Example 7b), according to their position in relation to the final, G.

Example 6. **nūbat al-aṣbahān, al-abyāt**

Example 6. (continued)

Example 6. (continued)

Example 6. (*continued*)

Example 6. (continued)

nūbat al-aṣbahān

al-abyāt
(*al-Turāṯ* 8:35)

yā ḏā allaḏī nabata al-ʻiḏāru bi-xaddihi
ka-l-barhamāni ʻalā sulūk il-jawhari
fa-ka'annahu al-miṣbāḥu fī ġasaq id-dujā
mutaʻallaqan bi-salāsilin min ʻanbari

O you on whose cheek the first growth of beard has sprouted
[You are] like the gemstone on the string of pearls
You are like a lamp in the darkness of the night
Hanging on chains of amber

a) El-Mahdi's scale of aṣbahān (el-Mahdi n.d.b. : 33)

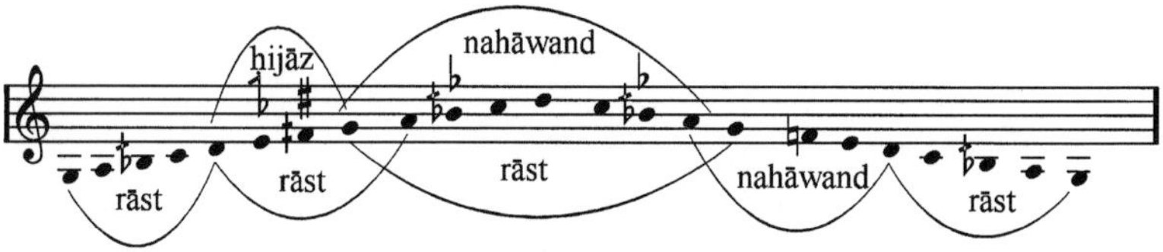

b) D'Erlanger's scale of aṣbahān (d'Erlanger 1949 : 368)

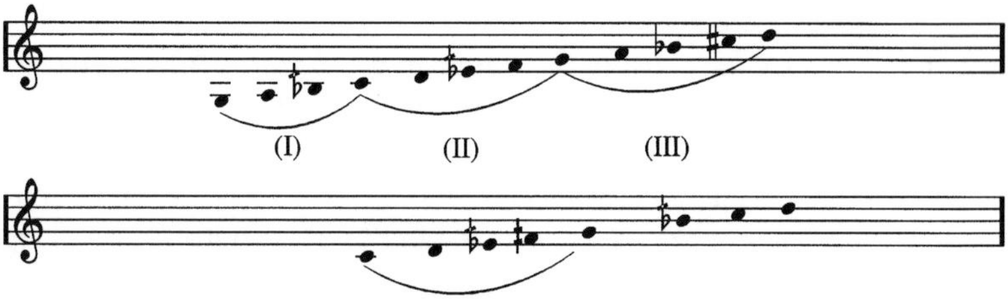

Example 7.

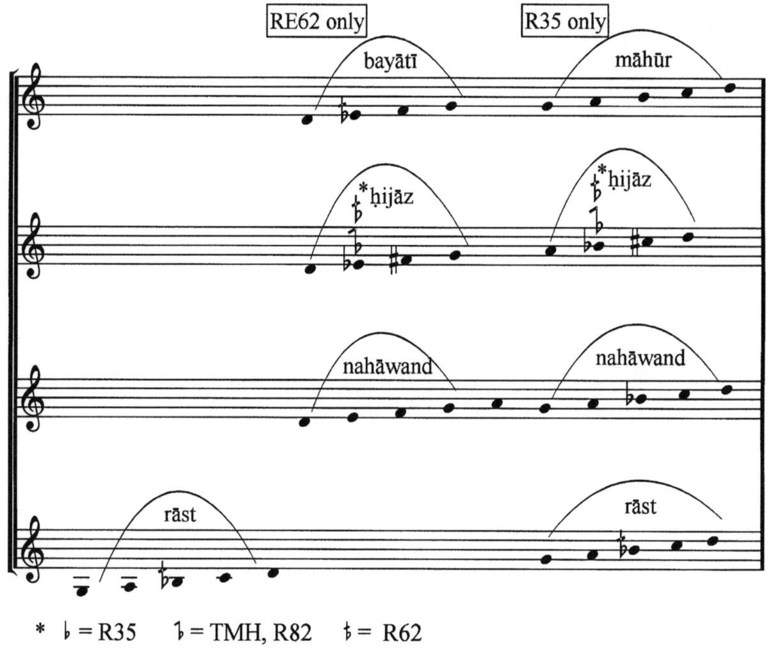

Example 8. ***The*** ᶜuqūd ***of the sources in Example 6***

THE FOUR VERSIONS COMPARED

Essentially, the four sources represent three melodic versions: (i) R35, (ii) TMH and R82, and (iii) RE62. Despite his insistence that his notations represented his personal interpretations, Saada's transcription (R82) corresponds in all but the slightest details to the published notations (TMH). A notable exception is the rhythmic variant in the progression from g to a on the last beat of m. 2 and the first of m. 3 (as in Belalgia's version, RE60).

None of the versions is consistent with either el-Mahdi's or d'Erlanger's scales alone. Thus, in all four sources, ^{c}*iqd* II is represented by both *nahāwand* on d (el-Mahdi's scale only) and by *ḥijāz* on d/c (el-Mahdi's/d'Erlanger's scales) but not by *rāst* on d/c (el-Mahdi/d'Erlanger's scales). At the higher register, the melody alternates in all four sources between *nahāwand* on g (el-Mahdi's scale only), *ḥijāz* on g (d'Erlanger's scale only), and *rāst* on g (both sources).

R35 is unique in omitting the signature 𝄳, thus apparently giving *mahūr* on g as the predominant ^{c}*iqd* on this degree. There does not seem to be any tradition of ^{c}*iqd mahūr* in *aṣbahān*, in theory or in practice, and it is likely that the omission of the signature was a copying error.

According to el-Mahdi, TMH should reproduce R35 virtually note-for-note with only superficial changes in order to simplify the rhythm and phrasing. There is a basic structural difference between R35 and TMH, however, in that R35 is the only version to set each *bayt* to a different melody. All three subsequent versions, including el-Mahdi's, omit the distinctive melodic setting in the repetition of *bayt* 1 (mm. 10–19) and instead, use essentially the same melodic setting for this and *bayt* 2 (mm. 19–28). There is a small deviation in Belalgia's version in that mm. 12–13 do not correspond to the equivalent passage (mm. 21–22, descending from *nahāwand* on g through *ḥijāz* on d) in bayt 2 but rather to the equivalent passage (mm 3–4, descending through *nahāwand* on d) in *bayt* 1.

As for el-Mahdi's claim to have simplified Triki's transcriptions, certain passages of relative melodic complexity in R35 are indeed presented more simply in TMH (see for example mm. 2–3, 5-8, 21–22); in certain other passages, however (e.g. mm. 1, 4–5, 10–11), the reverse is the case.

According to Belalgia, the most distinctive aspect of his version (R62) was the substitution of ^{c}*iqd ḥijāz* on d (mm. 5, 14 and 23) by ^{c}*iqd bayātī* on d. Despite Belalgia's insistence, however, that his interpretations were consistent with tradition, musicians of both the radio and Rashidiyya ensembles considered the inclusion of *ᶜiqd bayātī* in *maqām al-aṣbahān* as controversial at the very least; one described it as a "violation" of the tradition. In other respects RE62 corresponds closely to TMH (with the minor exception relating to mm. 12–13).

CONCLUSION

Since Tunisian Independence, two contrasting ideologies have emerged regarding the status of notation in the *maᵓlūf*. The official establishment view, represented by Salah el-Mahdi and embodied in the title of *Al-Turāṯ al-mūsīqī al-tūnisī* (*The Tunisian Musical Heritage*), is consistent with the ideology of a unified, national cultural identity. According to this view, the purpose of notation was to define and restore an essentially unitary tradition in which superficial deviations had occurred over the centuries as an inevitable result of oral transmission. Unlike the embellishments deliberately introduced in solo performance, such ingrained deviations were seen not so much as creative contributions but rather as corruptions or deformations, which the transcriptions would serve both to correct and prevent.[14]

Echoing this view, Mahmoud Guettat describes the Rashidiyya's "long work of recuperation and transcription . . . in order to safeguard the musical heritage (particularly the *maᵓlūf*) against every current of deformation, the erosion of time and the weakness of the collective memory . . ." (Guettat 2000: 240–41). Hamadi Hania, administrator in the *dār al-ṯaqāfa* (literally, house of culture; cultural centre) of Zaghouan,[15] gave the official ideology a popular twist when he described the Rashidiyya's notations as the pure, unadulterated version of the Andalusian melodies, restored to their original state after centuries of oral transmission and neglect under foreign (i.e. Ottoman and French) rule.

The official view was contested by both Abdulhamid Belalgia and Mohamed Saada, who in turn succeeded el-Mahdi as leaders of the Rashidiyya ensemble. These musicians regarded the variants characterizing the oral traditions as legitimate melodic attributes representing the personal contributions of successive generations of shaykhs. As leaders in a written tradition, therefore, they claimed a corresponding right to define their own interpretations of the melodies in notation. They also believed that the variable quality of the oral traditions, resulting from improvization, should be extended to the written tradition by periodically revising the notations.

Belalgia's and Saada's view was supported by the famous *maʾlūf* authority Tahar Gharsa. As the favored disciple of Shaykh Khemais Tarnane—the principal source of the Rashidiyya's notations, Garsa was generally considered Tarnane's "heir." He insisted that some of the melodies he had learnt from his mentor differed from the published versions and that he too cultivated his own melodic variants. Gharsa regarded it as his mission to pass on Tarnane's legacy to his own students and, when the opportunity arose, to transcribe and publish Tarnane's versions himself.

Evidently, however, the musicians did not always realize their ideologies in practice. If the versions represented in Example 6 are considered chronologically, the most substantial differences occur between Triki's and el-Mahdi's; ironically, of the three musicians represented since Triki, only el-Mahdi laid no significant claim to personal creativity. Meanwhile, Saada, who in our conversations described his own notations as "personal interpretations" and el-Mahdi's as "a collection of dead notations," virtually reproduced note-for-note el-Mahdi's version in *al-Turāṯ*.

Belalgia's version contains a striking personal contribution in his inclusion of *ᶜiqd bayātī* in *nūbat al-aṣbahān*; however, his notion that his interpretations are consistent with tradition was in this case unanimously contradicted by the views of other musicians. Nor did I find evidence that either Saada or Belalgia had put into practice their ideology of creating fresh notations for subsequent performances.

After some seventy years of continuous use, notation has not resulted in a definitive version of the repertory for the Rashidiyya ensemble: even if Saada and his successors pay no more than lip-service to the ideology of revising their interpretations there already exist at least three notated versions of *nūbat al-aṣbahān* in the Rashidiyya archive. Since Triki's transcriptions were themselves derived from performances they could never, by definition, be invested with an authority comparable to that characterizing notation in a written tradition. Their very conception was an act of compromise, the results arbitrary in their relationship to the various individual interpretations they replaced. Whether overtly or covertly, successive leaders of the ensemble have exploited the essentially arbitrary nature of the notations they inherited to justify their revision. Thus while notation was originally introduced to standardize the melodic tradition, it has since been used as a creative tool for reinterpreting and redefining it; and the fluidity of interpretation characterizing the oral traditions has not entirely been extinguished.

NOTES

1. Originally called *al-jamʿiyya al-rašīdiyya lil-mūsīqā al-tūnisiyya* (the Rashidiyya Association for Tunisian music) it was subsequently renamed *al-maʾhad al-rašīdī lil-mūsīqā al-tūnisiyya* (The Rashidiyya Institute for Tunisian music) and, in 1965, *al-maʾhad al-rašīdī lil-mūsīqā al-ʿarabiyya* (Guettat 2000: 240).

2. The Maghreb-wide movement of cultural and artistic "associations," or *jamʿiyya*, arose around the turn of the twentieth century, inspired by the various struggles for national independence. Dedicated to a variety of pursuits, including religion and sport, the *jam'iyya* were generally characterized by a spirit of openness to Western influences, modernization, and reform (Guettat 2000: 228–30). In Tunisia, the first musical associations were civilian bands modelled on the Western-style military band of the beylical court (see below) and the bands of the French occupation.

3. The standard Arab accidental signs (p. 12) were used to signify degrees between b and 𝄳 and between 𝄳 and #.

4. Since the nineteenth century, Western notation has been widely adopted throughout the Middle East as a theoretical tool, a means of documentation, a mnemonic aid to learning and, exceptionally, as a basis for performance. In general, the use of notation is associated with other aspects of Westernization such as European-style music academies and ensembles inspired by Western orchestral models. The Tunisian example is remarkable for the relatively early date that notation was integrated into regular performance and for the national scope of its use.

5. A manuscript containing transcriptions of the *maʾlūf* in Western staff notation, compiled by several army officers, is held in the archive of the Rashidiyya Institute (Zghonda n.d.: 8).

6. The female singer was the music theatrical star Chafia Rochdi.

7. Mohamed Triki (1899–1996) had studied the violin with a French priest at his *lycée* in Tunis, and he had conducted rehearsals of the French symphony orchestra of Tunis. His experience of the *maʾlūf* derived both from public performances in the *zawāyā* and private lessons with individual shaykhs, and he had studied Egyptian song with the visiting celebrities Kāmil al-Ḵulaʿī and Aḥmad Farūz. Triki had attended the classes given by Shaykh ʿAlī al-Darwīš on his visit to Tunis in 1931. Shaykh ʿAlī had apparently taken a special interest in Triki and given him private lessons.

8. Tarnane was the *ʿūd ʿarbī* player in the Tunisian ensemble at the 1932 Cairo Congress.

9. As a professional, contracted body, the membership of the radio *maʾlūf* ensemble, unlike that of the Rashidiyya, was fixed.

10. The singers, who were not required to read notation, continued to be recruited from the lay public as before. Many regarded the Rashidiyya chorus as an apprenticeship for a future career as a solo singer.

11. In an interview held immediately after the Tabarka congress, Triki upheld the official aim of the congresses to create a unitary national tradition by "arriving ultimately at a single method and style upon which all will agree." Like el-Mahdi, Triki maintained that the differences between the versions were not essential to the melodic substance but involved rather "differences in the styles of presentation and recitation, that do not go beyond adornment and embellishment" (Anon 1963: 26).

12. Établissement de la Radio-Télévision Tunisienne. Television was added in 1967.

13. I include transcriptions of the corresponding recordings by Belalgia and Saada and a transcription of the *abyāt* of *nūbat al-aṣbahān* by the Rashidiyya ensemble led by Salah el-Mahdi, made by Radio France in 1954, in Davis 1986a: 247–66. According to my transcriptions, the performances are virtually identical to the notated sources RE62, R80, and TMH respectively.

14. This view reflects d'Erlanger's arguments regarding the fallibility of oral tradition and the need therefore to introduce the musicians to musical notation (1949:337).

15. Mountain spa town some 70 kilometres south of Tunis; a traditional center of the *maʾlūf*.

Shaykh Ahmed el-Wafi. Old photograph of a painting by Rodolphe d'Erlanger. Louati 1995: 81.

Rodolphe d'Erlanger. Self portrait (detail). Louati 1995: 64.

Old postcard depicting a traditional maʾlūf *ensemble. Louati 1995: 81.*

Shaykh Khemais Tarnane at the 1932 Cairo Congress. Photograph provided by Salah el-Mahdi.

Photograph of the Tunisian ensemble at the 1932 Cairo Congress. CMAM 1992: 36.

Salayha. Star singer of the Rashidiyya, 1941-58. CD cover. CD 06. n.d.

Mohamed Triki, Salah el-Mahdi, and Khemais Tarnane. Photograph provided by Salah el-Mahdi.

The Rashidiyya in rehearsal (detail). Photograph by Ruth Davis, 1996.

Abdulhamid Belalgia, musical director of the ERTT, *in his office. Photograph by Ruth Davis. 1996.*

Tahar Gharsa playing ᶜūd ᶜarbī *at the Abou Nawas hotel, Tunis. Photograph by Ruth Davis. 1996.*

Tahar Gharsa and his ensemble singing the maʾlūf *at the Abou Nawas hotel, Tunis. Photograph by Ruth Davis. 1996.*

Street in Testour. Photograph by Ruth Davis. 2001.

Firqa *of the* ᶜĪsāwiyya *singing the* maᵓlūf *in a procession to the bride's home, Testour. Photograph by Ruth Davis. 2001.*

Sonia M'Barek. CD cover. AAA 186. 1999.

El-Azifet. *CD Cover. CD004. n.d.*

Lotfi Bushnak. Photograph provided by the artist.

Chapter Four

Cultural Policy and the *Ma'lūf* of Testour

Until Tunisian independence in 1956, the work of the Rashidiyya had no significant impact on *ma'lūf* traditions outside the capital. After independence, the *ma'lūf* was designated the national musical heritage and the Rashidiyya became the model and source for *ma'lūf* practices throughout the nation. At the same time, the new government adopted a negative attitude towards the Sufi brotherhoods, causing their musical traditions to be irrevocably undermined.

Although the *ma'lūf* was unknown to large sections of the population, it was in other respects relatively well qualified for its privileged status. As an urban musical tradition it was common at least to many communities, unlike the rural traditions, which were considerably more varied (Abdul-Wahhab 1918: 16).[1] As an Arab musical and literary repertory the *ma'lūf* reflected the government's policies to Arabize Tunisian culture; it had the prestige associated with the Arab-Andalusian heritage, and it had a legend that passed in both popular and scholarly imaginations as a history. But the *ma'lūf*'s most valuable asset was the fact that it had been systematically documented, studied, and presented by the Rashidiyya Institute. The government was merely left to assimilate the Rashidiyya's methods and achievements into its cultural and educational program. The Rashidiyya provided the government with a Tunisian musical repertory in notation, teaching, and performance models and a source of music teachers, administrators, and advisors. With the benefit of these resources and a new national network of cultural and educational institutions, the government extended the

Rashidiyya's efforts to conserve and promote the *ma'lūf* from their center in Tunis, throughout Tunisia.

THE NEW INSTITUTIONS

After independence the Western music conservatory, founded in Tunis in 1896, was converted into the National Conservatory of Music and Dance.[2] The *ma'lūf* became the cornerstone of the new music curriculum, which also included Middle Eastern and Western traditions; this was formalized by the presidential decree of 23 January 1958 specifying the requirements for the national diploma of Arab music.[3]

In 1961, a separate Ministry of Culture was established with the specific responsibilities of cultivating the national cultural heritage; providing a basic, popular education in all aspects of that heritage; and forging relations with foreign and international organizations (Said 1970: 19; Kacem 1973: 30). From the outset, the new Ministry's commitment to the Tunisian cultural identity was intrinsically linked with ideals of modernization and change, including receptivity to foreign influences. As Mahmoud Messadi, former Minister of Culture, explained, "cultural development must be considered both as a factor of the national—or cultural—identity and at the same time, as a means of transforming society and its civilization . . . the project of development and modernization is pursued under the triple banner of loyalty to one's own identity, the deep desire for improvement, and the wise and rational selection of external borrowings and influences to be integrated in the modernizing process" (quoted in Kacem 1973: 40).[4]

In pursuit of its goals, the Ministry of Culture created a nationwide network of cultural and recreational institutions called *diyār al-ṯaqāfa* (literally, houses of culture; s. *dār al-ṯaqāfā*; *maisons de la culture*) and *diyār al-šaʿab* (literally, houses of people; *maisons du peuple*) whose activities were co-ordinated by a parallel network of national, regional, and local cultural committees (Said 1970: 35–37; Kacem 1973: 38–40).[5]

The Ministry of Culture was divided into various specialized departments including a Department of Music and Popular Arts; this was directed by Salah el-Mahdi who, in 1949, had taken over from Mohamed Triki as leader of the Rashidiyya ensemble. El-Mahdi's ministerial position established him as Director of the National Conservatory, and he held both posts until 1979, when he was succeeded in them by his former pupil, Fethi Zghonda. During that period, el-Mahdi was personally responsible for the musical policies promoted by the government.

Throughout the 1960s and 1970s, the Ministry of Culture created a network of amateur music clubs and ensembles along the lines of the Rashidiyya and its school in the new provincial centers; it supplied these institutions with instruments, and it sent out graduates of the Rashidiyya and the National Conservatory to organize and teach the new ensembles using copies of the Rashidiyya's notations as sources. At the same time, the Ministry proceeded with the publication of the notations in the nine-volume series *al-Turāṯ al-mūsīqī al-tūnisī* which it distributed to the new ensembles (el-Mahdi 1981: 80; 83). Thus the *ma᾿lūf* was introduced to areas where it was previously unknown and unfamiliar versions of the melodies, styles of performance, teaching methods, and institutional contexts were introduced to communities where the repertory had traditionally been cultivated. Over the years, certain *diyār ṯaqāfa* developed systematic teaching programs along the lines of the National Conservatory; some, such as in Sfax and Sousse, became fully fledged regional conservatories offering the entire curriculum up to diploma level.

The Ministry of Culture established an annual cycle of *ma᾿lūf* competitions and festivals to encourage and monitor the new ensembles, culminating each summer in the national competition and festival of the *ma᾿lūf* in Testour (el-Mahdi 1981: 83). The adjudicators of the Testour festival were selected from the ranks of the Rashidiyya and the National Conservatory; the Ministry of Culture set the guidelines for the ensembles' programs, and it established the criteria by which their performances were judged.

According to Fethi Zghonda, el-Mahdi's successor as Director of Music and Popular Arts, the programs followed the standard format set by the Rashidiyya. Each ensemble performed an instrumental overture, or *baṣraf*, or an instrumental piece in a similar style. This was followed by a *nūba* or part of a *nūba*,[6] including a solo vocal or instrumental improvisation in the same *maqām*, a song from the *ma᾿lūf* outside the canon of *nūbāt*, an *'ugniyya* in a Tunisian *maqām*, and a new vocal or instrumental composition in the style of the *ma᾿lūf*. The ensembles were assessed according to instrumentation, intonation, vocal and instrumental technique, and melodic interpretation. The guiding principles for the choice of instruments were, according to Zghonda, correct intonation and balancing of timbres; thus for example, ten violins would need two to three cellos while five would need no more than one. Instruments of fixed pitch were unacceptable, while more than one *qānūn* was suspect because of the difficulties in synchronizing their tunings. Desirable interpretations were, Zghonda insisted, those based on the published notations.

Each winter, representatives of the various regional ensembles attended a week-long residential music course, run by teachers from the Rashidiyya and the National Conservatory, devoted to learning a *nūba* and other repertory of the *maʾlūf*.[7] Many ensembles performed the same repertory in the competitions they entered during the following months. Thus, throughout the year, ensembles throughout Tunisia were rehearsing and performing the same pieces from the standard repertory of the Rashidiyya according to the Rashidiyya's notations.

THE DEMISE OF THE SUFI FIRAQ

The new government considered the Sufi movement both politically suspect and socially regressive. During the Protectorate, certain Sufi leaders had cooperated with the French against the resistance movement; as a result, the government viewed the brotherhoods generally, with their loyalties to their *zawāyā*, with distrust. At best, they provided distractions from the national cause and at worst, they were potential sources of political opposition. Moreover, the Sufis' esoteric beliefs and customs, particularly the extreme physical practices they performed in trance, were considered shameful relics of a backward and oppressed society, counteractive to modernization and progress.[8] The government reacted by suppressing their extreme physical practices, confiscating their lands and other possessions, and generally denigrating the movement as outmoded and corrupt. Many *zawāyā* were converted into Neo-Destour party headquarters; others were closed and subjected to lengthy restoration programmes. As their activities were restricted and their social prestige plummeted, membership of the brotherhoods declined and, throughout the country, *zawāyā* emptied and ceased to function (Speight 66: 58; Jones 1977: 39–40). In some communities the *firaq* continued their traditional musical activities outside the *zawāyā*; but they operated in a social and spiritual vacuum that was scarcely alleviated by the alternative institutions provided by the government.

After its initial shock reaction the government began to modify its attitude toward the brotherhoods. An alternative view, represented by Salah el-Mahdi and supported by President Bourguiba, recognized some of their traditions, particularly their musical practices, as valuable and harmless representations of indigenous folklore that deserved to be fostered and preserved (Jones 1977: 40). While maintaining its official disapproval of the Sufis' trance activities, the government gradually relaxed its prohibitions and it attempted instead to integrate the Sufi musicians into its official cultural programs (Jones 1977: 38 ff.). Some groups gravitated towards the new cultural institutions while others returned to the *zawāyā* where they rehearsed under the auspices of the local *dār al-ṯaqāfa*.[9]

THE MAᶜLŪF IN TESTOUR

In the following pages I consider the effects of the government's policies on the *maᵓlūf* of Testour, a small agricultural town in the Medjerda valley about seventy-five kilometres northwest of Tunis. Testour was founded by Andalusian refugees in the early seventeenth century and, like other towns in the region, it has a strong *maᵓlūf* tradition;[10] its particular reputation rests on the fact that, since 1967, it has hosted the annual national festival of the *maᵓlūf*. My decision to focus on Testour was determined by my discovery in the archive of the ERTT of a unique collection of recordings featuring the *firqa* of the *ᶜĪsāwiyya* of Testour made by government officials shortly after independence. In addition to relgious songs, the recordings include most of the *nūbāt* of the *maᵓlūf*.[11]

Testour was chosen as the venue for the first national festival of the *maᵓlūf* as part of a general governmental policy to "decentralize" the national culture (Said 1970: 35). The main purpose of the festival was to promote the *maᵓlūf* among young people and, to this end, it took the form of a competition between the various regional ensembles. Around 1970, the Ministry of Culture launched an international exchange scheme to include musicians from other countries of the Maghreb, and a hotel was built to accommodate the foreign artists. Over the years, the festival expanded to include groups from the wider Middle East and Spain; however, despite the increasing internationalization, the national competition remained at the heart of the program, and the festival culminated each year with a broadcast performance by the Rashidiyya.

In June 1982, I attended the Testour festival as a guest of the Ministry of Culture. The performances took place in the evenings in the garden of the hotel where the foreign artists, adjudicators, and other official guests were staying. That year, the foreign participants included *maʾlūf* ensembles from Algeria and Libya and a Spanish flamenco dance group. Each day, fresh busloads of Tunisian ensembles were deposited at the hotel, only to depart at the end of the evening. Typically, they comprised an instrumental section of young men and boys playing from the published notations and a mixed chorus; occasionally, the instrumentalists included a lone girl on the *ʿūd* or *qānūn*. There were no representatives of *maʾlūf xam*.

The performances were presented on a colorfully decorated, brightly lit dais with banks of speakers on either side. The audience, mostly local townspeople, were seated in rows of chairs, stretching back into the darkness. That year, the festival coincided with the month of Ramadan and people were restless after the day's fasting; some shouted extravagant reactions, others sang along, while many caught up with the day's gossip, ignoring the performers altogether. Occasionally someone fainted from exhaustion.

The ensemble representing Testour comprised three violins, two cellos, an *ʿūd sharqī*, *naqqārāt*, *ṭār*, and *darbūka*, played by young men, and a chorus of six young men and girls. They were led by the *ʿūd* player, Mongi Garouashi. Mongi told me that the *firqa* of the *ʿĪsāwiyya* still performed *maʾlūf xam* at weddings and other communal celebrations but they had dissociated themselves from the youth ensemble and the festival. He invited me to return to Testour for a wedding later than month.

I revisited Testour several times during the following year, as a guest of Mongi and his family. I attended rehearsals of the youth ensemble in the *dār al-ṯaqāfa* and rehearsals and performances by the older musicians. The following account is based on the information I gathered during those visits.

*****

Shortly after independence the firqa of the *ʿĪsāwiyya* withdrew from the *zāwiya*, which was closed for an extensive program of repairs. In 1960, representatives of the government visited Testour to record its musical traditions, including most of the *nūbāt* of the *maʾlūf*. The recordings were stored in the archive of the ERTT; apparently no-one in Testour received copies. When the *dār al-ṯaqāfa* was built in the early 1960s, the *firqa* at first gravitated there to renew its rehearsals but the musicians felt uncomfortable in the strange environment, which lacked the atmosphere and traditions of the *zāwiya*. Their rehearsals decreased, their standards dropped, and their repertory declined. The *firqa* continued to accept new, younger members; however, without a venue, teaching had become an ad hoc affair that was mostly conducted in cafés and in private homes.

The older musicians began to demand payment for their performances at wedding celebrations that they had previously given freely, as an honor to the family and the community. They began to exclude the younger members so that there would be more money to go around. In the past, the membership of the *firqa* was fixed and spanned all social classes; by the late 1960s, it had dissolved into ad hoc assemblings of poor people seeking opportunities to earn money.

In 1969, two years after it had launched the Testour festival, the government provided the *dār al-ṯaqāfa* with musical instruments and a music teacher from Tunis. The teacher was a graduate of the National Conservatory and a violinist in the radio ensemble. According to Mongi, he had no interest in teaching the ensemble of Testour while, for their part, the older musicians took offence at being instructed in their own tradition by an outsider, and a young man.

In 1970, Mongi moved to Sfax, a large coastal town south-east of Tunis, where he had found a job as an engineer. Mongi became a part-time student at the music conservatory, where he was introduced to the published notations. He discovered that the printed melodies and texts were different from those he had learned in Testour.

When Mongi returned to Testour three years later, he found that the violinist from Tunis had retired from his post and the government had suspended its funds for a music teacher. Mongi felt a personal responsibility for the *maʾlūf* of Testour, and he took charge of the musical activities of the *dār al-ṯaqāfa* without payment. His aim was to create a modern *maʾlūf* ensemble that would, nevertheless, preserve the individuality of the Testour tradition, by integrating the older musicians with younger ones. The older musicians would impart their knowledge of the traditional repertory while the younger ones would learn the new musical instruments supplied by the government.

In the archive of the ERTT, I discovered a video fragment of a performance by the Testour ensemble in the 1976 Testour festival. The ensemble looked like the mixture of Sufi and modern elements that Mongi had described. The instrumentalists, dressed in white *jabāyib* and seated on a row of chairs, played three violins, *ᶜūd šarqī*, *nāy*, *darbūka*, and *naqqārāt*; all were young men or boys except for the *ṭār* player who was very old and seemed almost too feeble to strike his instrument: he sang along, stroking it irregularly. Mongi was playing the *ᶜūd*. Behind the instrumentalists, the chorus stood in a long straggling row. It comprised girls in dark skirts and white blouse, boys in dark trousers, white shirts, and bow ties, and men of mixed ages and dress including some very old men in *jabāyib*. The shaykh directed the chorus from the side, waving them in and beating time in the vocal sections and waiting passively in the instrumental sections.

Mongi's experiment was short-lived: the new standards and methods he had acquired in Sfax conflicted with those of the older musicians. Mongi transcribed the versions of the melodies that he had learned from the older musicians as a basis for teaching the instrumentalists. But the old men insisted on teaching the chorus in the traditional manner, remorselessly repeating passages that were too long for their pupils to remember. According to Mongi, they scarcely understood the words they sang; their renderings were grammatically incorrect, and they mispronounced the unfamiliar words. Mongi tried to correct their "mistakes" but after countless repetitions of Mongi's versions they reverted to their former habits. The ensemble performed in the Testour festivals of 1975 and 1976 and then dissolved. The young musicians formed a new ensemble under Mongi in the *dār al-ṯaqāfa*; the older musicians withdrew from the *dār al-ṯaqāfa* and the Testour festival, but they continued to perform for a fee at weddings.

The activities of Mongi's youth ensemble focused exclusively on the annual festival. The musicians usually began to rehearse their new programme a few weeks beforehand; afterwards the ensemble split up until the following summer. Mongi explained that he found it difficult to assemble the young people for rehearsals because of their incompatible schedules. The majority were either school children, who could not rehearse late at night, or students who attended institutions outside Testour; meanwhile, those who had jobs tended to work outside the town. Mongi himself had a full-time job as an engineer, which often took him away for several days. In 1983, about thirty people had volunteered to perform in the festival but only fifteen were sufficiently prepared to do so. Meanwhile, the old musicians rarely assembled during the winter since weddings were normally held in the summer. For most of the year there was no *ma'lūf* in Testour.

Mongi complained that the people of Testour generally were losing interest in the *ma'lūf*; his observations were echoed by others. Young people tended to display more enthusiasm for the latest hits of the radio and TV stars than for the *ma'lūf* of the Rashidiyya and the old men at weddings: there were no glamorous models for the *ma'lūf* to attract them. Over the past decade, people from outside the region had begun to settle there in search of work. The newcomers had imported their own musical traditions, including the *mizwid* (bagpipe with two single free-beating reeds), a popular urban instrument recently taken up by the mass media. The indigenous inhabitants were increasingly inviting the *mizwid* players to perform at their weddings after the old men had finished singing the *ma'lūf*.

The decline in support for the *ma'lūf* apparently extended to the nation as a whole. According to Mongi and officials in the *dār ṯaqāfa*, fewer ensembles were participating in the festival, and the standards were dropping. Some attributed the decline to a change in leadership style since the departure, in 1979, of Salah el-Mahdi as director of Music and Popular Arts. Apparently el-Mahdi's leadership had been characterized by a highly energetic personal involvement; for example, he was constantly on the phone to the leaders of provincial ensembles (normally, his former students) encouraging them in their efforts. The approach of his successor, Fethi Zghonda, in contrast, was more low key. Others blamed financial considerations: young people were generally more interested in learning potentially lucrative instruments such as the electric guitar, keyboard, drumkit, and violin, which they could use to accompany solo singers at weddings, than the *ma'lūf* and its traditional instruments, which had scant economic value.

The Testour Tradition and the Published Notations

After the older musicians had withdrawn from his ensemble Mongi began to prepare transcriptions that he described as syntheses, according to his taste, of the notations in *al-Turāṯ*, the versions he recorded off the radio, and the melodic traditions of Testour. He continued to teach both the singers and instrumentalists by the traditional method of repetition and memorization, singing, and playing on the *ᶜūd* the melodies he had transcribed. Occasionally he substituted the published versions of the texts for the Testour versions, correcting their grammar and pronunciation.

As an example of his method, Mongi showed me the notations of *nūbat al-aṣbahān* he had prepared for the ensemble's performance at the 1978 Testour festival. He had learned the Rashidiyya's version of the *nūba* at the residential music week the previous winter, and his own notations included the *abyāt*, previously unknown in Testour. However, instead of the *bṭāyḥiyya* normally sung by the Rashidiyya Mongi had transcribed the *bṭāyḥī "fī jannati'l firdawsī"* ("In the garden of paradise") traditionally sung in Testour. Apparently, this *bṭāyḥī* had never been recorded by the Rashidyya or the radio ensemble.

Example 9 compares Mongi's transcription of the *bṭāyḥī "fī jannati'l firdawsī"* of *nūbat al-aṣbahān* with the traditional Testour version and the published notations. This example gives the *bayt* (mm. 1–9/10) and the *talāᶜ* (mm. 11–19) for each source; the *rujūᶜ* is in each case a literal return to the *bayt*. The three versions are designated TMH, T60/83, and T78 as follows:

TMH The version notated in *al-Turāṯ* 8: 51–52.

T60/83 My transcription taken from the recording in the ERTT archive of *nūbat al-aṣbahān* sung by the *firqa* of the *ᶜĪsāwiyya* of Testour in 1960. This is virtually identical to my transcription taken from my recording of *nūbat al-aṣbahān* sung by the *firqa* of the *ᶜĪsāwiyya* of Testour in 1983.[12]

T78 Notations prepared by Mongi Garouachi for the performance by the Testour youth ensemble in the 1978 Testour festival.

The complete Arabic text, in both published (*al-Turāṯ* 8: 35) and sung (Testour) versions, is given in transliteration and English translation following Example 9. Example 10 shows the *ᶜuqūd* used in each source.

Example 9. nūbat al-aṣbahān, bṭāyhī 1

Example 9. (*continued*)

Example 9. (*continued*)

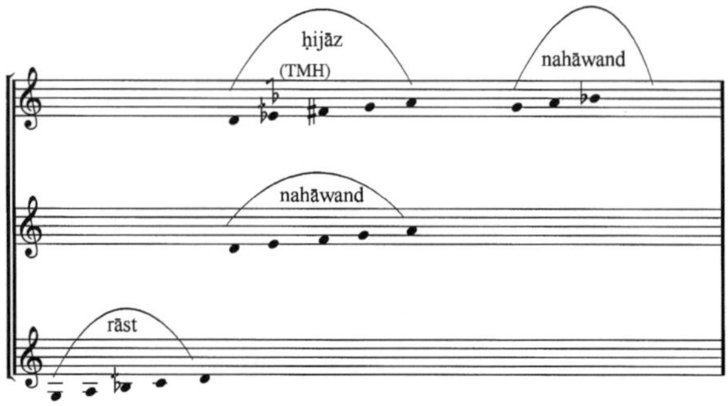

Example 10 The ᶜuqud of the sources in Example 9

1 The Traditional Testour Version (T60/83) and the Published Notations (TMH)

The two versions share the same progression of *ᶜuqūd* in the *bayt*. In the Testour version, however, *ᶜiqd ḥijāz* is only partially defined, lacking the characteristic third degree (f #) in m.3. In terms of melodic detail, TMH is denser and more complex (see for example m. 4 and the cadential passage mm 7–9).

In both the traditional Testour version and the published notations, the second half of the *talāᶜ* (mm. 14–18/19) replicates the second half of the *bayt* (mm. 5–9/10). In the first part of the *talāᶜ* (mm. 10/11–14), however, there are differences in the progression of *ᶜuqūd* between T60/83 and TMH. In the Testour performances, the *talāᶜ* ascends through *ᶜiqd nahāwand* (g-b) (m. 11) and descends through *ḥijāz* (g-d, m. 12) before returning to rest on *ᶜiqd nahāwand* (mm. 12–14). The corresponding section of TMH meanders up and down through *ḥijāz* (mm 10–12), before embarking on an elaborate descent from *ᶜiqd nahāwand* (m. 12) through *ᶜuqūd ḥijāz* and the *sīka* trichord of *rāst* (d—B𝄳) followed by an ascent through the same *ᶜuqūd* (mm. 13–14).

In sum, TMH is generally more elaborate than T60 and T83 in terms of surface detail, and it is also more dynamic in its contrasting of *ᶜuqūd* and tessitura in the *talāᶜ*.

2 Mongi's Version, (T78) the Traditional Testour Version (T60/83 and the Published Notations (TMH)

Mongi described his own notations generally as syntheses, according to his taste, of the Testour version, the published notations, and the versions

bṭāyḥī al-aṣbahān
(*al-Turāṯ* 8:35)

ṭāla'

fī jannati al-fīrdawsi ra'aytu al-quṣūra al-'ālīya
rāmī ramā b-il-qawsi ḥarbuhu bi-šafratin māḍīya

abyāt

yā hal turā man kān minhu bi-ḥāl ḥubbī malīḥ
yuḥarrak al-iskān wa yuġrī al-'aqla ar-rajīḥ
'ahyaf ẓarīf fattān mā fīhi 'ayb ilā šaḥīḥ

ṭāla'

yu'allalka bi-l-būs wa yahuzzu as-sumra al-'ālīya
rāmī ramā b-il-qawsi ḥarbuhu bi-šafratin māḍīya

ṭāla'

In the garden of paradise, I saw the high palaces
An archer aimed an arrow at me with his bow, his spear has a sharp blade

abyāt

O I wonder who there is who is as handsome as my lover
He stirs up the neighborhood and entices the serious mind
Most slender, elegant and charming, his only fault is stinginess

ṭāla'

He makes you ill with kisses, brandishing the tall lance
An archer aimed an arrow at me with his bow, his spear has a sharp blade

bṭāyḥī al-aṣbahān
Testour version

ṭāla‘

fī janna fī jannata il-firdawsa ra’ayta ḥūr il-‘ayn
rāmī rāmī ramā b-il-qawsa ḥarbah bi-šafra šafra māẓīya

abyāt

yā hal turā man kāna minhu bi-ḥāli ḥubbu malīḥ
yuḥayy yuḥayyarik il-makān wa yuġribu il-‘agla il-‘agla ar-rajīḥ
hayif hayif ẓarīf fattān mā fiha ‘aybun ilā šaḥ šaḥīḥ

ṭāla‘

yu‘allilik bi-l-būs wa yuhizzu is-sumra al-‘ālīya
rāmī rāma ramā-il-qawsa ḥarbah bi-šafra šafra māẓīya

ṭāla‘

In the garden of paradise, I saw the virgin of paradise
An archer aimed an arrow at me with his bow, his spear has a sharp blade

abyāt

O I wonder who there is, whose love is as nice as his
He makes you feel disorientated, and takes away your mind
He is slender, elegant and charming, his only fault is stinginess

ṭāla‘

He makes you ill with kisses, brandishing the tall lance
An archer aimed an arrow at me with his bow, his spear has a sharp blade

recorded by the Rashidiyya and radio ensembles; in the case of "*'fī jannati'l firdawsi*," however, no such recordings had been made.

In the *bayt*, Mongi's transcription paraphrases the melody of the traditional Testour version, retaining the same progression of *ʿuqūd*. The first half of Mongi's *talāʿ* likewise corresponds to that of the Testour version. However, instead of returning to the second half of the *bayt*, as in both the Testour and published versions, the second part of Mongi's *talāʿ* simply restates the first half. Overall, therefore, Mongi's version is clearly based on the traditional Testour version and the differences between them show no traces of the influence of the published notations.

In sum, in the case of "*fī jannati'l firdawsi*," the melodic tradition of Testour had remained essentially intact since independence. This was evident both in the performance of the older musicians I recorded and in the notations prepared by Mongi for a performance by the younger musicians, only five years earlier.

*****

Mongi frequently complained about the poor technique of the players; their intonation was unreliable and their phrasing was undisciplined, but he had no time to remedy these faults. Many of the instruments needed repairing or replacing, but he had neither the time nor the money to do either properly. Nor did he have time, any more, to prepare his own transcriptions. During the rehearsals I attended for the 1983 Testour festival Mongi taught directly from the published notations. The main item was *nūbat al-aṣbahān* and that year, Mongi's ensemble presented the standard program of the Rashidiyya, substituting the *bṭāyḥī "jismi fāni min hawāk*," recorded by both the Rashidyya and radio ensembles, for the *bṭāyḥī "fī jannati'l firdawsī*" traditionally sung in Testour.

Mongi believed that the *maʾlūf* of Testour was in danger of being entirely obliterated by the version "imposed" from Tunis. He thought that the only way to secure both its survival and its official recognition would be to provide it with a complete notated source, comparable to the Ministry's publications. However, he lacked the time to carry out such a project: he insisted that it would take the resources of a full-time music teacher to transcribe all the traditional melodies and to teach the ensemble to read notation so that they could perform them accurately. Meanwhile, Mongi's proposed project had suffered a blow with the unexpected death of Shaykh Mohamed ben Ismael, the last great shaykh of the *maʾlūf* of Testour, the previous year. Many traditional melodies were believed to have died with him.[13]

There was a widespread feeling among the local inhabitants that the government had exploited Testour: it had sent representatives to record their musical traditions, but it had not provided the musicians with copies, nor had it provided the *dār ṯaqāfa* with recording equipment of its own. It had sent them an incompetent music teacher without providing the funds to replace him. It had supplied them with musical instruments without providing the funds to maintain them. Every year, Testour hosted a festival that promoted *maʾlūf* ensembles from throughout the Mahgreb, yet the government had done little, they felt, to promote the *maʾlūf* of Testour.

NOTES

1. The third volume of Laade's three-volume anthology of his field recordings from Tunisia is devoted to rural traditions (Laade 1962c). In his extensive notes, based on information provided by Manoubi Snoussi, Laade lists some fifty different vocal genres.

2. *al-Maʿhad al-waṭani li'l mūsīqā wa'l raqs; Conservatoire National de Musique et de Danse.*

3. The contents of the decree are outlined in el-Mahdi 1981:71–74.

4. Tunisia's dualistic cultural aspirations mirror those of the Egyptian Ministry of Culture established in 1958, six years after the 1952 revolution. Egyptian cultural policy was based on the notion that "culture in Egypt must be based on exchange; the cultural heritage must be preserved and nurtured, but it must also be open to a situation of dialogue with influences from abroad" (Wahba 1972:17; quoted in El-Shawan 1984: 103).

5. The Tunisian institutional structures were apparently modelled on those of France where, two years earlier, de Gaulle had established the Ministry of Culture under André Malraux. Malraux's ideology of promoting a national culture was effected through a network of provincial *Maisons de la Culture*, centrally controlled from the capital (Born 1995:72); however, whereas in France, the aim of the national cultural policy was to popularize élitist culture, Tunisian cultural policy had, in the case of the *ma'luf*, the reverse effect among the majority of its practitioners. In Testour, for example, it transformed what was previously a grassroots popular tradition into an officially sanctioned academic tradition based on élitist models such as the Rashidiyya and radio ensembles.

6. A part of a *nūba* normally comprised a sequence of songs either in duple meter (*bṭāyḥiyya* and *brāwil*) or in triple meter (*adraj*, *xafāyif*, *axtam*).

7. The music course formed part of an annual cycle of residential courses called *semaines d'art*, organized by the Ministry of Culture, each devoted to a particular art or craft.

8. In her account of the music of the ᶜĪsāwiyya of Tunisia, Jones records certain practices "that regularly accompanied their *ḥaḍrāt* (ceremonies) in former times," including "eating nails, broken glass, hot coals and scorpions; rolling on a bed of cactus figs; putting sharp pointed objects through the flesh of the abdomen and face; lacerating themselves with swords and imitating the behaviour of certain animals." The ᶜĪsawiyya also cultivated snake-charming, healing, and exorcism (1977: 36–37). Jones claims to have witnessed all of these activities except for the eating of scorpions and rolling on cactus.

9. Jones observes that the rehabilitation of the brotherhoods was accompanied by varying degrees of secularization. In cases where the groups revived their traditional ceremonies, or *ḥaḍrāt*, the practices associated with trance were reduced to "an exceptional rather than a regular feature [. . . .] and with some *firaq* they practically never occur" (Jones 1977: 36–37). She elaborates, "their role as performing ensembles maintaining a branch of Tunisia's musical folklore has been emphasized, and people have been encouraged to cultivate their traditions in a spirit of musical professionalism and with a pride in their guardianship of the national cultural heritage . . . The official point of contact between the brotherhoods and the government is through the Ministry of Culture rather than the religious establishment, and the basis for this contact is in musicianship and the preservation of a cultural heritage" (1977: 41).

10. Architectural styles and family names suggest that the original inhabitants came from Aragon and Castille (Hamrouni 1974: 19).

11. The ERTT possesses no comparable collection of recordings from this period of any other provincial ensemble.

12. Since 1960, the musicians had performed under the same shaykh, rejected the input of the music teacher sent from Tunis and dissociated themselves from the *dār al-ṯaqāfa* and the Testour festival: not surprisingly, therefore, their traditional interpretation had remained unchanged, showing no influence of the published notations.

13. Shaykh Mohamed had represented Testour at the three national *ma᾿lūf* conferences organized by the Ministry of Culture in the early 1960s.

Chapter Five

The *Ma'lūf*, Popular Song, and the Mass Media

> It is widely accepted that in each major Near Eastern or Asiatic "high culture" one should expect to find a self-contained indigenous musical repertoire which is authentic, ancient, musically sophisticated and socially exclusive. Such a repertoire is usually described as "classical music," "art music," "court music," and "serious music." (Racy 1981: 4)

To the extent that it claims medieval Arab origins, it was cultivated by trained professional musicians in the beylical courts of Tunisia, it is a distinct repertory with a continuous history dating back more than a thousand years, and it is underpinned by a theoretical tradition that it shares with a broad complex of Arab, Persian, and Turkic court and urban genres, the *ma'lūf* would appear to qualify in conventional terms as an "art music" repertory. It acquired an academic status comparable to that of Western art music with the founding of the Rashidiyya Institute in Tunis in 1934.

In popular mythology, the *ma'lūf* is perceived as an uninterrupted legacy symbolically connecting contemporary Tunisian communities to the golden era of their Andalusian past. The published notations appear to support this myth by presenting the *ma'lūf* as a closed canon of mostly anonymous compositions. Recently, however, certain Tunisian scholars such as Belhassan Farza, Salah el-Mahdi, and Mahmoud Guettat have proposed a contrasting image of the *ma'lūf* as a historically layered, continually adapting and essentially open-ended repertory, reflecting a broadly-based Tunisian rather than an exclusively Andalusian identity. El-Mahdi maintains that, once transplanted in Tunisia, the *maʾlūf* absorbed so many indigenous elements as to become "almost purely Tunisian" (el-Mahdi 1981: 10).[1] Most of the song texts combine classical Arabic with Tunisian dialect, indicating that they were altered or even newly composed in Tunisia. The instrumental pieces of the *nūbāt* are conventionally attributed to the eighteenth century ruler Muḥammad al-Raŝīd Bey and, in addition to the *nūbāt*, the *maʾlūf* contains songs and instrumental pieces reflecting more recent Turkish and Middle Eastern influences (Guettat 2000: 303–04; 313–14; Farza n.d.: 12). Certain pieces in the published notations are attributed to particular twentieth century composers, including el-Mahdi himself, implying that the canon is still in fact open-ended.

Despite its courtly patronage, the *maʾlūf* was never primarily an elitist repertory. Its principal patrons were Sufi brotherhoods, whose membership spanned all social classes, while outside the zawāyā the *maʾlūf* was sung in a variety of communal contexts. Historically, therefore, the *maʾlūf* was "popular" in the sense of being "of the people" as a whole, rather than being confined to any particular social élite (Manuel 1988: 2).

When performed by solo instrumentalists and singers, whether in the beylical courts or in popular communal contexts, or by large synchronized ensembles such as the Rashidiyya, the *maʾlūf* does indeed require specialist expertise. *Maʾlūf xam*, however, demands no special skills other than the ability to memorize the songs, and membership of a Sufi *firqa* was traditionally determined by commitment to the *zāwiyya* and its activities rather than by specifically musical criteria.

Alongside its "art" music credentials, therefore, an equally valid historical profile emerges for the *maʾlūf* as a "popular" musical genre, in the sense that it was enjoyed by all social groups, its repertory was continually self-renewing and open to new musical forms and styles, and its performance could be unsophisticated enough for anyone to join in, regardless of talent, training, or expertise.

In this chapter I explore changes in the traditional status of the *maʾlūf* and its relationship with new composition that occurred with the rise of the mass media and the development of new types of popular song in the twentieth century. My account focuses on the period up to the mid-1980s, roughly coinciding with my first extended stay in Tunisia and the end of the first phase of Tunisian independence under President Habib Bourguiba.

GENESIS OF THE *MA᾽LŪF* CANON

> The death of a single shaykh of art approaches in its effect the burning of a library of manuscripts.
>
> Old Tunisian proverb cited by el-Mahdi (1981:79)

As an oral musical tradition, the *ma᾽lūf* depended for its survival on the memories of the shaykhs. Since the shaykhs held their positions by virtue of their superior knowledge of the repertory, they guarded their knowledge jealously: thus, when a shaykh died, it was believed that many songs died with him. At the same time, a shaykh's death provided opportunities for renewal. According to el-Mahdi, until Shaykh Ahmed el-Wafi broke the taboo in the early twentieth century, "composers were embarrassed to have their works attributed to them because people used to be biased towards the old [. . .] especially that which the Andalusian emigrants brought with them. As a result, each composer pretended that he had memorised his work from a dying shaykh who was its only source. He did that so that other singers would accept and perform it" (el-Mahdi 1981: 89).

The *ma᾽lūf* canon, as represented in al-Turāṯ, is conventionally divided into three broad chronological layers: (i) the songs of the thirteen *nūbāt*, in volumes 3–8, representing the original Andalusian core; (ii) songs and instrumental pieces reflecting Ottoman and broader Middle Eastern influences, believed to have been added anonymously from the mid-eighteenth to the early twentieth centuries, and (iii) repertory attributed to particular twentieth century composers.

Within the second layer, the collection of ten instrumental pieces called *bašārif* (s. *bašraf*) in volume 1, together with the instrumental pieces of the *nūbāt*, are traditionally attributed to the court of Muḥammad al-Rashīd Bey (d.1759).[2] Volumes 2 and 9 comprise songs that are excluded from the *nūbāt* on the basis of their *maqāmāt*, *iqā᾿āt*, and/or other structural and stylistic characteristics; these songs are arranged in groups of two to four called *waṣlāt* (s. *waṣla*, literally, chain). Many of the *waṣlāt*, particularly those in volume 9, mix songs of different *maqāmāt*, and certain individual songs are themselves based on more than one *maqām*.[3]

While most of the pieces in volumes 2 and 9 are anonymous, volume 2 contains two songs by Ahmed el-Wafi (d. 1921) and volume 9 includes two by el-Wafi, four by Khemais Tarnane (d. 1966), and one by

Mohamed Ghanem (the *rabāb* player of d'Erlanger's ensemble). The so-called *waṣlāt* 29, 30, and 31 in volume 9 are in fact three newly composed *nūbat*: *nūbat al-ḵaḍra* in *maqām al-nahāwand* is by Shaykh Khemais Tarnane and *nūbat ᶜajam al-ᶜušayrān*, and *nūbat al-zankūlāh* are by Salah el-Mahdi.[4]

Most of the songs in volumes 2 and 9 follow the same *bayt* and *qufl* structure as the songs of the *nūbāt* (p. 6). The exceptions are the four anonymous songs in volume 9 called *fūndū* (pl. *funduwwāt*; literally, "joyous"), which have a couplet/refrain structure; the individual couplets are frequently in different *maqāmāt*, and they are separated by vocal improvisations called *ᶜarūbī*.

Originating in the late nineteenth century, the *fūndū* is considered the prototype of the *ᶜuġniya tūnisiyya*—the dominant media genre of the twentieth century, likewise characterized by a couplet/refrain structure; indeed, two of the *funduwwāt* in volume 9 are subtitled *uġniya ᶜatīqa*, literally, "old song." According to Shakli, both the *fūndū* and, in its early stages, the *uġniya*, were intimately associated with performances of the *maᵓlūf*. *Funduwwāt*, which generally use only Tunisian *maqāmāt*, were sometimes incorporated into performances of *nūbāt*, while *maᵓlūf* ensembles around the turn of the century used to round off their programmes with a sequence of *funduwwāt* and *aġānī* in vogue (Shakli 1994: 180–81).

TWENTIETH CENTURY DEVELOPMENTS

1 Before Independence

Like d'Erlanger, Tunisians generally portray the early decades of the twentieth century as a period of decadence and decline for Tunisian music. However, while d'Erlanger blamed Western influences, Tunisians percieve the principal threat as coming from the East. Numerous scholars have described how Egyptian and other Middle Eastern celebrities pervaded the cafés and theatres of Tunis in the early years of the twentieth century and how, in particular, the successes of the Egyptian singer Shaykh Salāma Hijāzī and his music theatrical troupe in the Rossini Theatre, in 1914, led to the rise of clubs specializing in performances of Middle Eastern songs. Increasingly, Tunisian musicians were abandoning the *maᵓlūf* and imitating the Egyptians in their dress and dialect as well as in their music (el-Mahdi 1981: 23–24; Farza n.d.: 12, Shakli 1994: 52–55; Moussali 1992: 5–6).[5]

In 1908, Gramophone introduced commercial recording to Tunis under the label of its French company Zonophone. According to the Algerian scholar, Bernard Moussali, the new medium was regarded with great suspicion by the majority of Tunisian artists and shunned by the best. "Performers of art music [*ma'lūf*], Islamic religious singers and Jewish singers alike refused to collaborate [. . .] fearing the diabolical powers of the foreign machines which could potentially 'steal' their voices or corrupt the divine message. Their decision undoubtedly explains the virtual absence of the *ma'lūf* among the earliest recordings" (Moussali 1992: 5).

By 1910, however, when Gramophone launched its first catalogue devoted to Tunisian music, the original inhibitions had apparently subsided. The list of double-sided discs included a series of records by the Jewess Layla Sfez devoted to the *ma'lūf* and to Middle Eastern songs; Shaykh al-Sadik ibn Arfa singing *qaṣāid* on traditional Tunisian and Middle Eastern modes; Shaykh Hasan ibn Amran singing mystic hymns of the Sulāmiyya brotherhood and verses of the *qur'an*; monologues and comic sketches by the Jewish actor Kiki Guetta; an assortment of Tunisian, Egyptian, and Ottoman marches by the beylical fanfare; and unspecified performances by the Egyptian *qānūn* player Mursi Barakat and the "exquisite" Jewish singer Tayra Hakim from Damascus, both resident in Tunis (Moussali 1992: 6–8).

Moussali's study, focusing on recordings of Tunisian musicians up to the 1930s, demonstrates above all the eclecticism of the repertory, apparently reflecting the variety of live musical performance in Tunis: certainly, no single category emerged above any other to qualify as a genre of "popular" music associated specifically with the record industry. Rather, "the expansion of the record industry, the onslaught of Syro-Egyptian productions, the fashion for Tripolitanian (*tarabulsiyyat*) and Algerian (*dziriyyat*) tunes, the inflation of musicians' fees and the struggle to emulate, if not to surpass them, resulted in an increased variety of choice in the domain of Tunisian music, which had beome multifaceted" (Moussali 1992: 6).

Tunisian accounts, in contrast, focus not so much on the diversity of Tunisian musical production during this period but rather on its inferiority. Blaming the record industry for the corruption not only of

Tunisian music but of musical life in general, Mahmoud Guettat describes the professional musicians of the time as "a class of opportunists whose depraved behaviour and financial greed dragged the art of music and the status of the musician into a deplorable situation" (Guettat 2000: 238). El-Mahdi for his part accuses the record industry of promoting songs with trite, obscene, and linguistically corrupt texts, some of which degraded the Arabic language by mixing it with French (el-Mahdi 1981: 25). Echoing el-Mahdi, Mohamed al-Saqanji criticizes the songs of the time for their use of colloquial or "relaxed" literary Arabic, their lightweight themes, and their bacchic and erotic character (al-Saqanji 1986: 16–24; cited in Moussali 1992: 8–9).[6]

In 1928, the Lebanese company Baidaphone mounted a massive publicity campaign in Tunis, inviting top Tunisian artists, including the Jewish singer Habiba Msika, the pianist and *qānūn* player Mohamed Qadri, and the singer and *ᶜūd ᶜarbī* player Khemais Tarnane, to record in Berlin alongside musicians from other Arab countries, using state-of-the-art German equipment.[7] Baidaphone's 1928 catalogue lists Habiba Msıka in a series of Tunisian, Lebanese, Egyptian, and Syrian patriotic songs and Middle Eastern *qaṣāid*, including "*Mā lī futintu*" and "*Lī laḏḏatun*," originally recorded by Umm Kulthūm, traditional songs from Tripolitania and traditional Tunisian wedding and circumcision songs, with both ensemble and piano accompaniment;[8] Khemais Tarnane is featured in songs from the *maᵓlūf*, Middle Eastern, Tripolitanian, and Algerian songs, and improvizations in Tunisian modes on the *ᶜūd ᶜarbī*; and Mohamed Qadri appears playing "on an 'oriental piano' of unknown make [. . .] a veritable anthologie of Tunisian, Egyptian, and Ottoman instrumental pieces" (Moussali 1992: 12–13).

According to el-Mahdi, Baidaphone's high profile project had a pivotal impact on the future of Tunisian song. On the one hand, it provoked a further upsurge of inferior musical production "causing havoc in the market of composing and writing and a collapse of taste to a dangerous degree . . ." On the other, it was their experience in Berlin that forced the Tunisian delegates to recognise their lack of a specifically Tunisian repertory suitable for recording (el-Mahdi 1981: 90).

Tunisian scholars generally present the founding of the Rashidiyya as the culmination of a rescue operation initiated by Tunisian musicians, only subsequently to be consolidated by the efforts of d'Erlanger and his circle (Farza n.d.: 12; el-Mahdi 1981: Guettat 2000: 238–40). El-Mahdi describes how Tunisian youth in particular reacted in defense of their music, believing that its very identity was under threat and that in order to save it "it was necessary to know it, probe its depths, preserve a part of its heritage, and study its *maqāmāt* and its *iqāʿāt*." He lists some of the great shaykhs who responded to these young men's needs, including shaykhs of the ʿAzūziyya and the ʿĪsāwiyya brotherhoods, and the shaykhs of instrumental ensembles who turned their homes into private clubs and schools for the *maʾlūf* (1981: 26–27). Thus when, in 1932, the Cairo Congress recommended that institutions be established throughout the Arab world to conserve and promote the indigenous musical traditions, this served merely as "fuel for the fire for those interested in Tunisian music since they had been thinking for a long time about the creation of an organization for that goal" (el-Mahdi 1981: 28).

The Rashidiyya aimed not only to rescue Tunisian music but equally to "rehabilitate musical activity as a whole" (Guettat 2000: 238); effectively, it replaced the commercial imperative of professional musicians by the moral imperative of dedicated amateurs. Subsidized by the government and presided over by the mayor of Tunis, the Rashidiyya provided for the first time a public, secular environment for Tunisian music comparable in social status and function to a Western music academy. In Tahar Gharsa's view, the fact that such an environment was dedicated specifically to the *maʾlūf* was consistent not only with the high quality of its music and poetry but also with the prestige associated with the Andalusian heritage and the respect traditionally enjoyed by the *maʾlūf* as the only secular repertory admitted into the *zawāyā*.

In its efforts to create songs of the highest quality the Rashidiyya held competitions, and it commissioned songs from its own poets and composers. According to el-Mahdi, the artists approached their work not so much as a recreation but rather as a duty. "All writers and musicians perceived their great responsibility and the need to correct the situation [. . .] to bring change to Tunisian music" (el-Mahdi 1981: 90). Mourad Shakli describes the spirit of disinterested amateurism that prevailed among the poets "convinced at once of the nobility and the urgency of their task"; many songs were created spontaneously in the context of informal evening gatherings of poets, composers, and singers (Shakli 1994: 255–56).

Unlike the *maʿlūf*, which was sung by the chorus throughout, the new songs (*aġānī*) featured a solo singer alternating with the chorus in the refrain.[9] The Rashidiyya demonstrated its commitment to the new songs by appointing the charismatic Chafia Rochdi, star of the musical theatre and the only female member of the founding ensemble, as its lead singer.

When she retired in 1941, Rochdie was replaced by the now legendary Salayha, considered to represent all that is quintessential in Tunisian song. Salayha sang with the Rashidiyya until her death in 1958.

The ensemble gave public concerts in the courtyard of the Rashidiyya on Saturday afternoons; their atmosphere was informal, more like a club, as the same audiences returned each time (el-Mahdi 1981: 58). Texts were passed round for the audience to sing along. A typical program comprised a *bašraf* or *bašraf sammāʿi*; a *nūba* or part of a *nūba* in the same *maqām*; one or more miscellaneous songs from the *maʾlūf* or a new song in a similar style; and a light strophic song, or *'uġniya*. Guettat observes that the tradition of fortnightly concerts "did a lot to raise the moral status of musical activity: as Mohamed Triki remarked, 'we went along as though to the mosque'" (Guettat 2000: 241–242).

When the Tunisian radio station was established in 1938, it appointed as it artistic director Mustafa Bushushah, brother-in-law of the Rashidiyya's president, Mustafa Sfar. The Radio adopted a policy to promote Tunisian music and artists and, at first, the Rashidiyya more or less monopolized its music programs; later, two evenings a week, eventually one, were devoted to live broadcasts of the ensemble while several of its artists broadcast independently on other evenings. During the decades leading up to independence in 1956, the Rashidiyya provided the springboard for some of the most popular media artists of the time including the now legendary female singers Chafia Rochdi, Salayha, Fathiya Khayri, Oulaya, Naama, and Shabila (daughter of Salayha). Today, songs of these and other media stars of the 1930s to the 1960s, many of whom sang with the Rashidiyya, are often loosely designated *maʾlūf*.

For musicians associated with the Rashidiyya, the *maʾlūf* is the foundation of all subsequent Tunisian composition: they refer to it variously as "the base," "the cradle," and even "the bread and butter" of Tunisian song. Despite their frequent introduction of Middle Eastern modes, rhythms, and styles the new songs promoted by the Rashidiyya in the last decades of the Protectorate were created by musicians and poets steeped in the *maʾlūf*; the old and new repertories were performed in the same programs, to the same audiences, by the same musicians and singers. Far from representing opposing tendencies, as implied in the familiar art/popular paradigm of Western music, the old and new songs were perceived as a continuum, the older repertory providing the inspiration, if not always the musical models, for the new.

2 After Independence

After independence a gulf emerged once more between the *ma˒lūf* and the new songs promoted by the mass media. A major factor behind this division was the creation, in 1958, of a full-time salaried radio ensemble. Modelled on contemporary Egyptian film and radio orchestras the new ensemble adopted the basic line-up of the Rashidiyya with the addition of European instruments such as flutes, clarinets, saxophones, accordions and, from the late 1960s, electric keyboards and guitars; synthesisers were added from early 1980s (Shakli 1994: 201–3).

The original members of the radio ensemble were drawn substantially from the Rashidiyya and graduates of its school; in addition, the Egyptian violinist ᶜAtiyah Šarārāh was brought in to lead the instrumentalists, and the Egyptian *qānūn* player, Fahmī Awād, was hired to train the chorus in Egyptian *muwaššahāt* (el-Mahdi 1981: 57–58). As full-time government employees the radio musicians no longer had time for unpaid rehearsals with the Rashidiyya, and the amateurs and professionals split. The Rashidiyya replenished its membership from among the teachers and advanced students of the Rashidiyya school and National Conservatory, and it continued in its traditional amateur status under el-Mahdi and others, subsidized by the Ministry of Culture and the Municipality of Tunis.[10]

With the founding of the radio ensemble, the Rashidiyya ceased to give regular live broadcasts. Instead, the ERTT created an archive of recordings, by both the Rashidiyya and a special reduced section of the radio ensemble, which provided the sources for its weekly programs of the *ma˒lūf* (el-Mahdi 1981: 58). Effectively, the ERTT created a recorded canon complementing the notated canon produced by the Ministry of Culture.[11]

In other respects, the radio ensemble pursued an independent agenda that looked primarily to Egypt for its sources and models. Its principal function was to accompany solo singers in recordings of popular Egyptian and new Tunisian songs. The ERTT selected the artists, it commissioned the songs, and the recordings were made in its own studios. Thus, until the advent of private recording studios in the early 1980s, the radio ensemble virtually monopolized the production of new Tunisian songs.

The radio ensemble's bias towards Egyptian music was reflected in the catalogues of the commercial cassette companies that emerged in the late 1970s. In 1983, both the two privately owned companies, Mallouliphone (Tunis) and La Societé de la Cassette (Carthage), and the state-owned Ennaghem, relied almost entirely on contracts with Middle Eastern companies, devoting approximately 5% of their output to Tunisian artists. The only company to have released recordings of the *maʾlūf* was Ennaghem: these constituted a handful of vinyl records based on the archival recordings of the ERTT.

When I began my fieldwork in Tunis in the early 1980s, musicians, journalists, and politicians alike were lamenting the "crisis" in Tunisian song. The *maʾlūf* was virtually confined to the Rashidiyya, the National Conservatory and the *diyār al-ṯaqāfa* and the only regular public performances were the monthly concerts of the Rashidiyya. On radio and television, the *maʾlūf* was relegated to weekly programs based on the original archival recordings of the ERTT. Meanwhile, the new songs promoted by the ERTT, also known as *mūsīqā xafīfa* (literally, light music) or derogatively, *mūsīqā "sandwich,"* were relentlessly derided as feeble imitations of their Egyptian counterparts.

There was a general sense of nostalgia for the era before independence—considered the golden age of Tunisian song when, in the last decades of the nationalist struggle, the best poets, composers, and singers, backed by the media, were united in their efforts to counter the pervasive influence of Egyptian music and "corrupt" Tunisian songs by creating an authentic Tunisian voice. As they lamented the passing of those stars and debated how to fill the vacuum, musicians and audiences alike blamed the Rashidyya and its spin-off state institutions, the music clubs and conservatories, with their uniform interpretations and sterile performance conventions, for turning the *maʾlūf* into a museum piece, removed from "real life" experience.

Mohamed Saada, leader of the Rashidiyya since 1979, was attempting to address these complaints by revitalizing the ensemble's repertory, performing pieces that had been neglected for decades, and commissioning new ones. At the same time, leading establishment musicians such as Salah el-Mahdi, Fethi Zghonda, and Rashid Sellami, director of the adult section of the National Conservatory, were expressing renewed interest in the use of traditional *maʾlūf* instruments such as the *ʿūd ʿarbī, naqqārāt*, and *rabāb*, and proposing a return to soloistic ensemble formats. More radically still, el-Mahdi and Sellami were advocating that solo instrumentalists learn the melodies aurally, by the traditional method of repetition and memorization, using the notations merely as prompts. By thoroughly absorbing the repertory in this way, they argued, the musicians would be equipped to improvise embellishments in a manner that was both personal and consistent with tradition.[12]

During the academic year 1981–82, el-Mahdi and Sellami jointly founded a *ma°lūf* ensemble in the adult section of the National Conservatory with the aim of putting their revisionist ideals into practice. The ensemble, which comprised an *ᶜūd ᶜarbī, rabāb*, muted violin, *nāy*, *ṭār*, *naqqārāt*, and a male solo singer, rehearsed weekly, led alternately by el-Mahdi and Sellami.[13] In the rehearsals I attended the instrumentalists had copies of the notation on stands. The leader played each phrase on the *ᶜūd*, el-Mahdi from memory and Sellami from notation, and the musicians repeated the phrases exactly, referring to their notations as prompts. There was no evidence of improvization either in rehearsals or performance: the ensemble's performance of *nūbat al-ḏīl*, which won second prize at the 1982 Testour festival, corresponded note-for-note to the published version.[14]

Rashid Sellami believed that the Rashidiyya itself should abandon its traditional format and divide into several small ensembles performing in rotation; instead of one concert a month, he explained, four ensembles would each give one concert a week. That way there would be "more *ma°lūf* to go round" and the ensembles would still have time to learn new programs. His view, however, was contested by Abdulhamid Belalgia, leader of the radio ensemble. Belalgia defended the large ensemble format, insisting that the key to restoring the popularity of the *ma°lūf* depended rather on promoting "professional" standards of performance, education, and research. He considered it anomalous that the Rashidiyya, the nation's principal ensemble for the *ma°lūf*, was designated "amateur"; indeed, Belalgia maintained that the only medium competent to perform the *ma°lūf* was his own "professional" radio ensemble. He proposed to prove this by re-recording all the *nūbāt* using fresh notations: he was only waiting for the ERTT to provide adequate studio facilities.

The wheel had turned full circle: the very methods and ideals that were originally devised to defend the *ma°lūf* against the "corruptive" influences of Egyptian music and the mass media were, fifty years later, being blamed for its demise.

NOTES

1. According to Belhassen Farza, the thirteen "Andalusian" *nūbāt* served as the "ideal model" for the repertory's subsequent development and enrichment by Tunisian composers (Farza n.d.: 11).

2. The Tunisian *bašārif* are a heterogeneous collection: each is structurally unique. Guettat observes that "the Maghrebian *bašārif* bear absolutely no relationship to the Egyptian *bašārif*," themselves modelled on the modern Turkish *pesrev*. The Tunisian genre, he points our, respects neither unity of *maqām* nor unity of *īqīᶜ* and both the number of sections (*xānāt*) and the number of rhythmic cycles in each section vary from one composition to the next (Guettat 2000: 314). An eleventh "*bašraf*," entitled "*šanbar*" after its rhythm, is attributed to Shaykh Khemais Tarnane.

3. There are eight *waṣlāt* in volume 2 and thirty-one in volume 9. The eight *waṣlāt* in volume 2 are based on *maqāmāt* of the Tunsian *nūbāt*, namely *rāst al-ḏīl* (nos 1–3); *ḥsīn ᶜajam*, *ḥsīn ᶜušayrān*, and *ḥsīn ṣabā* (4–6); *al-aṣbaᶜayn* (7) and *sīka* (8). Songs in the Tunisian *maqāmāt mḥayyar sīka*, *mḥayyar ᶜirāq*, *ᶜajam ᶜušayrān*, and *ᶜajam* that are based on the rhythms of the *nūba* are considered to be fragments of "lost" *nūbāt*.

4. *Nahāwand* and *zankūlāh* are Middle Eastern *maqāmāt*. The first "new" *nūba*, by Khemais Tarnane, was composed for Victory day on 1 June 1955 and broadcast on Independence day on 20 March 1956. Salah el-Mahdi's *nūbat ᶜajam al-ᶜušayrān* was broadcast on the second anniversary of independence in 1958 (el-Mahdi 1980: 56–7).

5. The vogue for Egyptian music affected musicians of all calibres and persuasions, including those associated with the *maᵓlūf*. Shaykh Ahmed el-Wafi, considered in *maᵓlūf* circles "*le musicien tunisien modèle*" (Guettat 2000: 239) influenced subsequent generations of Tunisian composers with his synthesis of Tunisian and Middle Eastern styles (Farza n.d.: 12; Guettat 2000: 239). Shaykh Khemais Tarnane, a pupil of el-Wafi, began his career by singing Middle Eastern songs and playing the *ᶜūd šarqī*, and he continued to use Egyptian *maqāmāt* and *īqāᶜāt* in his compositions for the Rashidiyya. Catalogues of the Gramophone company dating from 1929–32 list Mohamed Triki, veteran composer and the original leader of the Rashidiyya, interpreting a "modern" repertory combining Tunisian modes, rhythms, and forms with Middle Eastern orchestration (Moussali 1992: 15).

6. Moussali notes the hypocrisy of such criticisms. Given that the *maᵓlūf* was equally characterized by erotic and bacchic themes and by the use of colloquial and relaxed literary language: "*pourquoi donc accepter dans le maᵓlūf ce que l'on refuse dans les chansons de l'époque?*" (Moussali 1992: 9).

7. The company was founded in Beirut, in 1907, by two Greek Orthodox cousins called Baida.

8. Habiba Msika was accompanied in her Middle Eastern songs by the ensemble from Baghdad comprising the Jewish *ᶜūd* player ᶜAzzūrī Hārūn al-ᶜAwād (Ezra Aharon), the Jewish *qānūn* player Sion Cohen, and the Christian violinist Jamīl Iskandar. Baidaphone had invited the Iraqi musicians to Berlin with the celebrated Baghdadi vocalist, Muhammad al-Qubbānjī.

9. Mohamed Triki explained that the distinctive performance practice for the *ma᾿lūf* was specifically designed to distinguish the older repertory from the new media songs.

10. The ERTT in contrast was controlled by the Ministry of Information.

11. An equivalent collection of video studio recordings was made when television was introduced in 1967.

12. Zghonda, in contrast, denied that the use of notation was an obstacle to improvization; on the contrary, he maintained that notation supported improvization by providing it with a uniform base, and that the ability to improvize correctly depended not so much on the method of learning the melodies but rather on a proper understanding of *maqām* theory.

13. The musicians complained that the rehearsals were too infrequent to be effective.

14. I am grateful to Rashid Sellami for providing me with a copy of his recording of this performance.

Chapter Six

Voices of the Nineties

In this chapter, I present various alternative approaches to the *maʾlūf* and the traditional repertories associated with it that emerged or acquired renewed prominence in Tunis in the early 1990s. The alternative approaches arose in a climate of mounting dissatisfaction with the established norms; and they went hand in hand with new directions in cultural policy favoring increased decentralization and the dismantling of unitary nationalist agendas. The concept of the *maʾlūf* as an emblem of national identity, forged by the Rashidiyya and adopted by the previous government at the heart of its cultural policy, gave way to a variety of more fluid, personal approaches to the tradition.

On 7 November 1987, thirty years after he had led Tunisia to independence, President Habib Bourguiba was officially declared senile and, in a bloodless coup, succeeded by Zine El Abidine Ben Ali. This landmark event, known as *al-Taġrir* ("The Change"), heralded a new political era, providing common point of reference for subsequent developments in Tunisian society. Musical commentators, however, tend to attribute the new approaches of the 1990s not so much to policies adopted in the wake of "The Change" but rather to a gradual shift in attitudes toward individualization and diversification which, they claim, had begun to occur up to a decade earlier. They cite as examples the renewed interest within the musical establishment in improvization, "authentic" instrumentation, and soloistic ensembles (pp. 100–101), and the emergence, in the early 1980s, of private recording studios breaking the monopoly of the ERTT (Sakli 1994: 340–42).

For some, the Tunisian cultural developments had a wider significance. Fethi Zghonda, head of music in the Ministry of Culture through the 1980s and much of the 1990s, presented the Tunisian situation as part of a global trend towards decentralization following the collapse of the Soviet Union and its cultural and economic models. In Tunisia, he observed, as in the wider Middle East and the former Soviet bloc, musicians were responding to the new ethos by returning to past performance models, picking up the threads of older practices before the era of state control.

In the following pages, I outline certain political and institutional developments relating to the *maʾlūf* in the years immediately following 'The Change.' I then sketch five high-profile projects representing contrasting approaches to the *maʾlūf* and its related repertories, featuring leading musicians and singers in Tunis in the 1990s.

POLITICAL AND INSTITUTIONAL DEVELOPMENTS

On 22 June 2000, designated the annual National Day of Culture, President Ben Ali delivered a speech to the nation outlining the ideological basis for the developments in cultural policy since "The Change." After confirming his intention to increase the state budget for culture Ben Ali reminded his audience that, in the new market economy, "culture belongs to everyone; its promotion is a collective responsibility." According to his "new vision of culture" this constituted "an important component of the production and marketing system," and he appealed to investors and business people alike "to take greater interest in this vital sector and lend support to the national effort."[1]

Since 1987, the monopoly previously held by the various state institutions on music education and amateur music making had been broken by an upsurge of private initiatives. In 1988, the award-winning violinist Amina Srarfi,[2] daughter of the eminent composer and lead violinist of the Rashidiyya Kaddur Srarfi (d. 1977), established the first private music conservatory in Tunis. Since then, a plethora of private conservatories have appeared in and around the capital and in other main towns. These typically offer the same basic curriculum, leading to the national diploma of Arab music, as the state conservatories; and, in many cases, they employ the same teachers, but each claims its own character, emphases, teaching methods, and specializations. A parallel development are the private music clubs—informal, amateur musical gatherings, generally led by established musicians specializing in particular types of repertory. The clubs are often attached to private conservatories and many support a professional ensemble. The most prestigious club for the *maʾlūf* is that of the veteran *ʿūd ʿarbī* player and chorus master of the Rashidiyya, Tahar Gharsa, who co-directs a private conservatory with his son Zied.

In 1990, the Ministry of Culture took a definitive step towards "denationalising" the *maʾlūf* by withdrawing its support for the annual national *maʾlūf* competition—previously the central component of the Testour festival and its original *raison d'être*. At the same time, the Ministry suspended the program of cultural exchange that had previously supported the foreign ensembles. The funds formerly allocated to prizes and adjudicators were diverted towards the hire of professional Tunisian ensembles, and the festival's organizers were encouraged to seek private sponsorship for any additional funds needed. As a result, the festival began increasingly to feature performers who had no particular connection to the *maʾlūf* and, apart from the continuing visits of the Libyan ensemble,[3] the international component ceased. Meanwhile, youth ensembles throughout the country were deprived of the main focus of their efforts and, in many cases, the major incentive for their commitment to the *maʾlūf*.

As it withdrew its support for the *maʾlūf* from the provinces, the Ministry of Culture consolidated its efforts in Tunis. In November 1992, it inaugurated the Centre des Musiques Arabes et Méditerranéennes in d'Erlanger's former palace, Ennajma Ezzahra, whose ownership had passed to the Tunisian government four years earlier. In its idyllic clifftop setting, surrounded by gardens and waterways, the CMAM houses the national sound archive; it hosts exhibitions and promotes research on various aspects of Tunisian music, particularly those relating to d'Erlanger's interests; it produces recordings of the *maʾlūf* and other traditional repertories; and it presents public concerts on themes relating primarily to the *maʾlūf* and to past and present personalities of the Rashidiyya.

In 1992, after several turbulent years marked by leadership crises and financial disputes, the Rashidiyya ensemble acquired a new leadership and a new professional status. On the pretext of raising the standards of the national *ma'lūf* ensemble the Ministry of Culture provided sufficient funds to appoint Abdulhamid Belalgia, retired leader of the radio ensemble, as the new leader of the Rashidiyya, and Tahar Gharsa its chorus master. As had occurred before, when Belalgia was appointed leader of the Rashidiyya in the 1970s (p. 56), the conservatory professors and students who had made up the bulk of the "amateur" ensemble were replaced by professional radio musicians; effectively, once again, the Rashidiyya was transformed into a specialist branch of the radio ensemble.

Today, apart from its leadership, the majority of the ensemble claims no special interest in or commitment to the *ma'lūf*. Originally an association of amateurs, united in their dedication to conserve and promote traditional Tunisian music, the Rashidiyya is now just another job and the *ma'lūf* just another repertory for a large proportion of its rank and file players.

FIVE CONTRASTING APPROACHES

1 Tunisie Anthologie du Ma'lūf

> *L'utilisation des instruments a cordes d'origine européenne a coté des instruments traditionnels et la fixation de la musique nécessaire aux grandes formations . . . n'ont nullement trahi l'authenticité de cette musique grace notamment a la perpetuation des formes mélodiques et des ornements qui en sont spécifiques.'* (Zghonda 1999: no page number)

For the Rashidiyya, the criteria for "authenticity" in the *ma'lūf* were, from the outset, essentially melodic. The radical expansion of the ensemble in the 1930s, with its unprecedented instrumental doublings, its emphasis on bowed string and choral timbres in both upper and lower registers, and its exclusion of the solo voice, was considered legitimate in that it in no way threatened the melodic integrity of the tradition; instruments of fixed pitch were excluded only because they compromised the integrity of the *maqāmāt*. The Rashidiyya's view thus contrasted that of d'Erlanger and indeed, the majority of the European delegates to the 1932 Cairo Congress, for whom authenticity in Arab music resided as much in the quality and balance of the vocal and instrumental timbres as in the melodic substance itself.[4]

The Ministry of Culture gave renewed impetus to the Rashidiyya's lush instrumental and choral sonorities through the 1990s in a series of recordings produced jointly with the Maison des Cultures du Monde

(Paris) entitled *Tunisie Anthologie du Malouf*. The first four volumes, subtitled *enregistrements historiques*, were released in 1992–93; these reproduce the original archival recordings of the radio *maʾlūf* ensemble based on transcriptions made by its leader Abdulhamid Belalgia. The fifth volume, in contrast, produced in 1994, features a contemporary performance of *nūbāt al-sīka* by a reduced ensemble (p. 17), which nevertheless retains the characteristic bowed string and choral sonorities of the Rashidiyya, led by Fethi Zghonda; his performance includes the seven songs discussed in Chapter One, reproduced in Example 4 according to el-Mahdi's notations in *al-Turāṯ*. Zghonda's recording, however, is based not on the published notations but rather on his own transcriptions, which he describes as "a synthesis of the transcription made by the Rashidiyya . . . and the version recorded by the Tunisian radio orchestra in the early sixties."

The sixth and latest contribution to the series, produced jointly by the Ministry of Culture and the CMAM in 1999, is a recording of *nūbat al-ḥsīn* by the Rashidiyya ensemble, conducted by Abdulhamid Belalgia. This performance is based on Belalgia's notations.

Evidently, for both Belalgia and Zghonda, the concept of authenticity transcends any single melodic rendering. When the Rashidiyya embarked on its transcription project in the 1930s, the very notion of melodic tradition was fluid and variable. The original transcriptions were understood to be authoritative but not definitive: their primary purpose was to unify the diverse interpretations of the shaykhs in order to create a viable performance practice for the newly enlarged ensemble. The very need to make the transcriptions arose out of the historic diversity of the oral tradition—a fact exploited by successive leaders of the ensemble to justify the validity of their alternative versions.[5] It was only after independence, under the influence of nationalist ideology, that the concept of a unitary national tradition took root and the published notations were promoted throughout Tunisia as the sole "correct" version of the melodies.

The concept of a "unitary" tradition, fixed in notation, was simultaneously undermined, however, from within the musical establishment by Abdulhamid Belalgia, who prepared his own notations for his recordings of the radio *maʾlūf* ensemble in the early 1960s. The authority of his versions, Belalgia claimed, derived from his extensive personal experience of the *ma'luf* traditions of the *zawāyyā* of Tunis in the years before independence. Thirty years later, Fethi Zghonda who, as Director of Music in the Ministry of Culture, had upheld the exclusive authority of the published notations, nevertheless created his own transcriptions for his official recording of *nūbat al-sīka.* Zghonda's versions, in turn, were rooted in the notated *maʾlūf* traditions of the post-independence establishment, as represented by both the Rashidiyya and the radio ensemble.

Significantly, it was Belalgia's recordings of the radio ensemble rather than el-Mahdi's of the Rashidiyya that had formed the main substance of the ERTT's *maʾlūf* programs since independence, providing not only a sound ideal but also, alternative tools for learning. Singers such as Lotfi Bushnak (see below), who generally received no formal musical education and could not read music, typically learnt the *maʾlūf*, not from the notations in *al-Turāṯ*, but rather, from tapes of Belalgia's recordings copied from the radio.

2 The Club of Tahar and Zied Gharsa and the Lineage of Shaykh Khemais Tarnane

For musicians and audiences alike, the undisputed bastion of authenticity for the *maʾlūf* in Tunis today is Tahar Gharsa. Born in 1933, Gharsa was a student of the Rashidiyya where he became the favored disciple of the Rashidiyya's original chorus master, Shaykh Khemais Tarnane (d. 1966). Tarnane was a student of Ahmed el-Wafi, the original mentor of the baron Rodolphe d'Erlanger; together, el-Wafi and Tarnane had served as d'Erlanger's sources for the Tunisian traditions in *La Musique Arabe* (d'Erlanger 1949: xv). Tarnane is recognized as the leading *maʾlūf* authority of his generation; he played the *ʿūd ʿarbī* at the 1932 Cairo Congress; he was the principal source of the Rashidiyya's original transcriptions, and he was one of the Rashidiyya's leading composers. Among connoisseurs of the *maʾlūf*, Tahar Gharsa is Khemais Tarnane's "heir."

As a solo singer and *ʿūd ʿarbī* player, Gharsa's reputation for authenticity rests in specific aspects of his vocal and instrumental style. These include the proper Tunisian pronunciation of individual words, the correct division of syllables, nuances of vocal and instrumental articulation, and details of melodic embellishment. Gharsa is also recognised as the only remaining master of the *ʿūd ʿarbī*—the four-stringed Tunisian lute, characterized by a more robust sound than the Egyptian *ʿūd šarqī,* which has almost totally replaced it. Exceptionally for a musician of his reputation and status, Gharsa has consistently pursued an independent career as the leader of small solo instrumental ensembles performing at private functions, such as weddings and circumcisions, and at informal venues such as cafés and hotels, eschewed as "vulgar" by the Rashidiyya. Famous for his radio recordings and live appearances, Gharsa has never made a commercial recording.

When I first met Gharsa in 1983, he told me that his mentor, Khmais Tarnane, had taught him many songs that had been neglected by the Rashidiyya and radio ensembles. Some had not been included in the published notations and of those that were, Tarnane's versions were frequently different, both in their melodies and their texts. Gharsa believed that some day, he personally would have the opportunity to bring this unfamiliar repertory to light. Meanwhile, he was teaching Tarnane's versions to his youngest son Zied, whom Tahar hoped would succeed him as master of the *maᵓlūf*.

Sixteen years later, in 1999, Tahar founded a private conservatory and a club for the *maᵓlūf* with his son Zied, in a rented villa in El Manar, a suburb of Tunis.The club meets on Friday evenings from about 6:30 to 9:30 in a spacious studio on the upper floor, carefully furnished by Tahar. At one end of the room, a display of heavy mahogany furniture, including a bookcase with fake leather-bound volumes, a bureau, a coffee table, and a gilded crimson plush sofa with matching chairs, creates the impression of a bourgeois salon; an antique record player with a brass horn and framed photographs of Tahar's family, interspersed with legendary personalities of the *maᵓlūf,* on the walls, complete the picture. Tahar, with his *ᶜūd ᶜarbī*, commands the room from the center of the sofa, his ensemble of some five or six musicians forming a semicircle around him. Among them, his son Zied plays either the viola or *rabāb*.[6] Facing the musicians, some two dozen regular participants sit in rows of classroom chairs with folding tables; they include men and women of various ages and diverse occupations, each drawn to Tahar's club by their love for the *maᵓlūf*.

When Tahar rehearses the chorus of the Rashidiyya, he liaises with Belalgia on matters of repertory and melodic interpretation. In his club, in contrast, he teaches his own and Khemais Tarnane's versions of the melodies, and he concentrates on lesser known repertory, including songs outside the published canon that he learnt from Tarnane. The chorus sing from photocopies of Tahar's handwritten texts, and they learn the melodies by the traditional method of repetition and memorization: Tahar sings each phrase in turn, accompanying himself on the *ᶜūd ᶜarbī*, and the chorus repeat it.

During the interval, the chorus retires and small glasses of sweet tea with pine nuts are passed round for the musicians, accompanied by plates of sweet and savoury pastries made by Mrs Gharsa. As the evening progresses the atmosphere becomes rapturous as the singers gain in confidence and the players improvize embellishments; occasionally, the room falls silent as one or other player breaks out into a full-scale solo improvization.

*****

On one of my visits to Tahar's club, in the spring of 2001, Tahar volunteered to record his own and Tarnane's version of the *barwal* "*mā bīdū qaḍiyya*" ("Man cannot help it") from *nūbat al-ḥsīn* so that he could demonstrate the differences between them. It was Tahar's choice of song, and I recorded him singing the two versions in succession, accompanying himself on the *ᶜūd ᶜarbī*.

Example 11 compares my transcriptions of the first *bayt* of Tarnane's and Gharsa's versions with the published version (*al-Turāṯ* 5: 72). There are no conspicuous differences between the three versions in the *ṭālaᶜ* and in each version the *rujūᶜ* recapitulates the melody of the *bayt*.

As shown in the Example, Tarnane's version is similar to the published version. The conspicuous melodic differences between Gharsa's and Tarnane's versions are shown in boxes.

3 "Lotfi Boushnak: Malouf Tunisien"

In the ensembles led by Gharsa, as in the traditional instrumental ensembles before the Rashidiyya, the solo singer and instrumentalists color the melodies with spontaneous embellishments and subtle nuances of articulation. The Rashidiyya, in contrast, with its thick string and choral textures and its use of notation to define every melodic detail, inhibited such channels of personal expression. Since the 1990s, certain high-profile singers have at once rediscovered and transformed the soloistic format, using the traditional melodies as vehicles for their individual vocal styles.

In 1993, the Maison des Cultures du Monde in Paris produced the CD entitled *Lotfi Boushnak: Malouf Tunisien*, featuring the Tunisian media star, famous throughout the Arab world for his eclectic range of Tunisian and Egyptian styles. Boushnak performs three *waṣlāt*, or abbreviated *nūbāt* (*al-aṣbaᶜayn*, *rāst al-ḏīl*, and *sīka*) singing solo throughout,

Example 11. *Nūat al-ḥsīn, brawal 6,* bayt *1*

barwal al-hṣīn
(al-Turāṯ *5: 53)*

TMH

mā bīdū qaḍīya	il-'abdu miskīn mā lū ixtiyār
il-hawā aḍnā fu'ādī	wa al-ġarām 'aḏḏab qulaybī
yā šam'a ḍawayya	insī mutayyam afnā-hu as-sahar

Tarnane

yā raytu qaẓīya	
mā bīdū qaẓīya	il-'abdu misakīn mā lū ixtiyār
il-hawā aẓnā fuwādī	al-ġarām māziq qulaybī
yā šam'a ẓawīya	wāsil 'ubaydik afnāhu s-sahr

Gharsa

yā yā bidū qaẓīya	
mā bīdū qaḏīya	il-'abdu misakīn mā lū ixtiyār
il–hawā aaaahhh fuwādī	al-ġarām māziq qulaybī
yā šam'a ẓawīya	wāsil 'ubaydik afnāhu s-sahr

barwal al-hṣīn
(al-Turāṯ *5: 53)*

TMH

The decision is not his, the slave is poor, he has no choice
Love consumed my heart and passion tortured my little heart
O bright candle,
Keep company the man enslaved by love, exhausted by sleepnessness

Tarnane

O I saw a problem
The decision is not his, the slave is poor he has no choice
Love consumed my heart, passion is ripping apart my little heart
O bright candle,
Come close to your little slave, exhausted by sleeplesssness

Gharsa

O the decision is his
The decision is not his, the slave is poor he has no choice
Love, aaahhh my heart, passion is ripping apart my little heart
O bright candle,
come close to your little slave, exhausted by sleeplessness

backed by an ensemble of nine solo instrumentalists on violin, *nāy*, *qānūn*, *ᶜūd*, cello, double bass, *naqqārāt*, *darbūka*, and *ṭār*.

Born in Tunis in 1954, Boushnak describes himself as an "autodidact:" like most Tunisian singers (as opposed to instrumentalists) he had received no formal musical education and he does not read music. He learnt the *maᵓlūf* in the choruses of the youth ensembles that rehearsed in the National Conservatory and the Maison de Culture "Ibn Khaldun" in Tunis, and from the canonic recordings of the Rashidiyya and the radio ensembles, taken from the radio. Boushnak began incorporating songs from the *maᵓlūf* into his solo repertory in the early 1990s; his 1993 CD recording was an initiative of the Maison des Cultures du Monde, inspired by a recital he gave there. The CD was followed by cassettes for the Tunisian market and by the mid-1990s, Boushnak's renderings of the traditional love-songs could be heard blasting from the cassette stalls along the Avenue Bourguiba in Tunis, blending with the latest hits of rival stars.

If Boushnak's soloistic interpretations seem like a throwback to traditional practice, as represented by Tahar Gharsa, this impression is misleading. Gharsa accompanies himself on the *ᶜūd ᶜarbī* and his solo voice alternates with a chorus provided by the instrumentalists. Boushnak, in contrast, maintains the strict separation between vocal and instrumental forces established by the Rashidiyya, and he dispenses with the chorus altogether, his voice alternating with the instruments alone.

Boushnak does, however, adopt a distinctive instrumental backing for the *maᵓlūf*, using only string and traditional Arab instruments in contrast to the electric guitars, keyboard, and drum kit he uses in contemporary songs. He also takes care to pronounce the words in the correct Tunisian (as opposed to Egyptian) way. In other respects, though, Boushnak makes no claim to authenticity, a fact acknowledged by his audiences. He insists that he has his own style influenced by no other singer or teacher: a chorus master can teach the "*grandes lignes*," he explains, but the expressive nuances that constitute a singer's personal style are his alone.

Unlike Gharsa, Boushnak has no special commitment to the *maᵓlūf*, itself a relatively recent addition to his repertory, or to its related popular traditions. And while Gharsa sings mainly to Tunisian audiences, preferably in informal settings, Boushnak, a jet-setting star, confines his public appearances to prestigious, high-profile events such as gala concerts and international festivals. When I last met him in his studio in Tunis, in April 2001, Boushnak told me that he had had enough of the archaic love songs whose romantic imagery and sentiments, he insisted, had no relevance for today's world: "*je ne suis pas un guardian du patrimoine*." Yet, he did not propose to abandon the *maʾlūf* altogether. He told me that he was composing a new *nūbat al-sīka* with contemporary lyrics in collaboration with the Tunisian poet Adam Fethi.

4 Sonia M'Barek: *Tawchih* and *Takht*

Like Lotfi Bushnak, Sonia M'Barek is a popular media star known for her innovative renderings of the *maʾlūf*. When I visited her in April 2001, her voice was heard daily on Tunisian radio, and her name was known to every taxi driver I rode with in Tunis.

Born in Sfax in 1969, M'Barek learned the *maʾlūf* and other traditional Tunisian songs from her grandmother before embarking on formal studies at the National Conservatory, where her teachers included Tahar Gharsa and Salah el-Mahdi, among others. She claims to be highly discriminating in her choice of repertory, focusing on traditional Egyptian and Tunisian songs, including the *maʾlūf*, and new songs by selected Tunisian composers. Her musical tastes, she explains, reflect her personal identification with Tunisian culture and history, and she considers the *maʾlūf* an important part of that identity. M'Barek is equally discriminating in matters of venue: she eschews hotels, weddings, and other private functions, where she could earn "*milliards*," and performs only in public concerts, where the music is "for listening." Like Boushnak, M'Barek claims to have her own vocal style, influenced by no-one in particular. She agrees that unlike Tahar and Zied Gharsa, her style is not particularly Tunisian; rather, she personalizes the *maʾlūf*, singing the songs in her own way.

In 1997, the CMAM produced a cassette entitled *Tawchih* (literally, "ornament") featuring M'Barek in a twenty-minute extract from *nūbat al-aṣbaᶜayn* (entitled *waṣlat al-aṣbaᶜayn*), a sequence of *muwaššahāt* from the *maʾlūf* in *maqām sīka*, songs by the veteran composers of the Rashidiyya Shaykh Khemais Tarnane and Mohamed Triki, and a new song by the young Tunisian composer Abdelhakim Belgaied. In this recording, M'Barek's supple, full-bodied, caressing voice is offset by a light instrumental backing of violin, *nāy*, *ᶜūd*, *qānūn*, cello, *riqq*, and *darbūka*; like Bushnak, she sings without chorus.

Tawchih was released on compact disc in 1999 by Club du Disque Arabe (Artistes Arabes Associés). In the same year, World Network produced

Takht (literally, "platform," the term used to designate the traditional solo instrumental ensemble of urban Arab music). *Takht* features M'Barek with the same line-up as *Tawchih* in a live concert recording at the WDR-Funkhaus in Cologne, in June 1998. In addition to the song by Belgaied and the extract from *nūbat al-asba'ayn* featured on *Tawchih*, *Takht* includes solo renderings of *waṣlat al-sīka*, *al-kurdi*, and *al-ḥsīn*, a *sammāᶜī*, and a new song by the Tunisian composer Mohamed Mejri.

With their English titles and extensive notes in French and English (*Tawchih*) and German, French, and English (*Takht*) M'Barek's CDs are clearly aimed at non-Arab audiences. M'Barak sees her own future direction in "world music," which in her view, embraces the concept of "authenticity" in the general sense of "expressing the character of a particular people or place." Criticized by some Tunisian purists for her improper pronunciation of the texts and her "exaggerated" expression, M'Barek has scored considerable successes abroad. Not only is the small solo ensemble format more practical and commercially viable for foreign tours; paradoxically, the clear, solo textures of the predominantly Arab instruments and M'Barek's expressive vocal style both appear more authentic and are also more aesthetically appealing to Western audiences than the large Westernized orchestras and choruses of the Rashidiyya and other establishment ensembles.

5 Amina Srarfi and El ᶜAzifet

In March 1992, the accomplished violinist and pioneering conservatory director Amina Srarfi challenged the virtual exclusion of female instrumentalists from the major state ensembles by forming her own all-female ensemble El ᶜAzifet (literally, "the female instrumentalists"). Srarfi's ensemble claims to be "the first all-female orchestra of Oriental and Tunisian music in Tunisia and in the Arab World as a whole" (Anon. 1998).[7] In conversation, Srarfi presents El ᶜAzifet as the modern counterpart of the female professional ensembles that traditionally entertained female audiences for wedding celebrations in private homes—a custom that apparently continued in Tunis until the early twentieth century. However, to the extent that El ᶜAzifet gives public performances to mixed audiences, its members are conservatory trained and musically literate, and most pursue professions outside music, the ensemble is indeed unprecedented. It comprises about twelve to fifteen women dressed in traditional Tunisian costumes, playing violins, a double bass, and Arab instruments such as the *ᶜūd, qānūn, nāy, darbūka* and *ṭār,* led by Amina Srarfi on the violin. The instrumentalists play from notation and they double as chorus; there is no solo voice. The ensemble performs in concerts and festivals all over Tunisia and it has made numerous trips abroad, in Europe, North America, and the Middle East.

Srarfi's ensemble specializes in the repertory with which her father, Kaddur Srarfi, was broadly associated. Apart from the *maʾlūf*, this includes "*chansons franco-tunisiennes*" of the 1920s and 1930s, in a mixture of French and Tunisian Arabic dialect; songs from the same period by the Jewish singers Cheikh El Afrit and Habiba Msika;[8] songs of Hedi Jouini, characterized by gypsy and Spanish influences, including the use of castanets; and songs by the "best" composers of the Rashidiyya such as Khemais Tarnane, Mohamed Triki, Ali Riahi, Salah el-Mahdi, and Kaddur Srarfi. Srarfi transcribes the songs directly from recordings in the ERTT archive and then adapts them for performances by her ensemble.

She describes the essential purpose of El ᶜAzifet as twofold: first, to prove that Arab Islamic women can perform as well as their male counterparts (a fact, she maintains, that Tunisian men will never acknowledge); and second, to prove that they can succeed independently of men. Derided by some as a gimmick, or specifically, an establishment ploy to present a liberated image of Tunisia to foreign audiences, El ᶜAzifet and its younger offshoots fulfill a unique and arguably necessary role in Tunisian music. Despite enjoying equal educational opportunities in the conservatories, where they equal or exceed the standards of their male peers, hardly any female instrumentalists and no female conductors have been accepted into any of the major professional or specialist ensembles established since independence.

In response to her detractors Srarfi points out that, unlike other establishment ensembles, El ᶜAzifet receives no subsidy from the government.[9] And far from being a one-off gimmick, El ᶜAzifet seems to have started a trend: since its founding, several members of the group have broken away to found all-women ensembles of their own.[10]

NOTES

1. I am grateful to Fethi Zghonda for providing me with a copy of the English transcript of the President's address.

2. Amina Srarfi was awarded first prize in violin at the National Conservatory in 1985.

3. The *ma᾿lūf* ensemble of Shaykh Hassan Araibi from Tripoli.

4. Jihad Racy analyses the ideological premises underlying the opposing Arab and European attitudes towards Westernisation, and the use of Western instruments in particular, in Racy 1991. I summarise Racy's analysis in my account of the Cairo Congress from the Tunisian perspective, in Davis 1993.

5. El-Mahdi himself acknowledged that the notations he used as leader of the Rashidiyya, which formed the basis of the published notations, were not identical to Triki's original transcriptions (pp. 56–57).

6. As Tahar approaches his 70th birthday, Zied is increasingly taking over his father's role as lead singer, in club sessions and in concerts, gradually acquiring the reputation of Tahar's "heir." Some critics, however, have reservations about the authenticity of Zied's vocal style; Zied himself acknowledges that this has been influenced by the closely related *ma᾿lūf* tradition of Constantine, Algeria.

7. In her ground-breaking study of "Tunisian Women as Professional Musicians," L. Jafran Jones observes that, in public musical life in Tunisia, as elsewhere in the Arab world, "women are singers while instrumental music and musical creation remain the domain of men" (Jones 1987:77).

8. Songs from this period, denounced as decadent by the Rashidiyya's founders and subsequently, by its official historians, have recently make a nostalgic comeback.

9. Srarfi acknowledges, however, the encouragement and promotional opportunities she receives from the Municipality of Tunis and the Ministries of Tourism and Culture.

10. The most well-known of these, Taqassim, rivals El ᶜAzifet in national and international reputation.

References

Abassi, Hamadi. 2000. *Tunis Chant et Danse 1900–1950*. Tunis: Alif—Les Éditions de la Méditerranée et les Éditions du Layeur.

Abdul-Wahab, Hassan Husni. 1918. "Le Développement de la Musique Arabe en Orient, Espagne et Tunisie," *Revue Tunisienne* 25: 106–117.

——. 1966. "Taqqaddam al-mūsīqā fi-l-šarq wa-l-andalus wa-tūnis" (Introduction to the music of the Orient, Andalusia and Tunis), *Waraqāt* 2, Tunis: 171–285.

Anon. 1963."Sayakūn la-na maᵓlūf muwaḥḥadun" (We shall have a Unified *Maᵓlūf*), *al-Iḏāᶜa* 10/5 (12/8/63): 24–27.

Anon. 1998. Notes to *El ᶜAzifet*. Direction Amina Srarfi. SOCA Music, SODACT CD004.

Born, Georgina. 1995. *Rationalising Culture*. University of California Press.

Boudhina, Mohamed. 1992. *Diwān al-maᵓlūf* (Anthology of the *Maᵓlūf*). Hamamet: Manšūrāt Mohamed Boudhina.

——. 1995. *Mūsīqā al-maᵓlūf* (The Music of the *Maᵓlūf*). Hamamet: Manšūrāt Mohamed Boudhina.

Danielson, Virginia. 1996. "New nightingales of the Nile: popular music in Egypt since the 1970s," *Popular Music* 15/3: 299–312.

Davis, Ruth. 1986. *Modern Trends in the Maᵓlūf of Tunisia, 1934–1984*. PhD diss., Princeton University.

——. 1993. "Tunisia and the Cairo Congress of Arab Music, 1932," *The Maghreb Review* 18/1–2: 135–44.

——. 2001. "Mode V.2. Middle East and Central Asia: *Maqām, Makam*." In S. Sadie and J. Tyrrell, eds., *The New Grove Dictionary of Music and Musicians*. 2nd Edition. London: Macmillan 16: 831–37; 858–59.

D'Erlanger, Rodolphe. 1917. "Au Sujet de la Musique Arabe en Tunisie," *Revue Tunisienne* 24: 91–95.

——. 1930–59. *La Musique Arabe*. 6 vols. Paris: Libraire Orientaliste Paul Geuthner.

——. 1933."Al-Maqāmāt al-muqaddamah min janāb al-bārūn di arlangar" (the *Maqāmāt* presented by the Honorable Baron d'Erlanger). In *Kitāb al-Mu'tamar* . . . . Cairo: 182–329.

Farza, Belhassen. n.d. "Al-Mūsīqā al-tūnisiyya fi'l qaran al-ᶜašrīn," ("La Musique Tunisienne au XXe Siècle). In *al-Turāṯ* 6: 3–12.

Guettat, Mahmoud. 2000. *La Musique Arabo-Andalouse. L'Empreinte du Maghreb*. Paris: Éditions El-Ouns.

Jones, Lura JaFran. 1977. *The ᶜĪsāwiyya of Tunisia and their Music*. Ph.D. diss., University of Washington.

——. 1987. "A Sociohistorical Perspective on Tunisian Women as Professional Musicians." In *Women and Music in Cross-Cultural Perspective*, ed. by Ellen Koskoff, 69–83. Urbana: University of Illinois Press.

Kacem, Abdelaziz. 1973. "La Politique Culturelle Tunisienne," *Annuaire de l'Afrique du Nord*: 29–44.

KMAA. 1933. Kitāb al-mu'tamar al-mūsīqā al-ᶜarabiyya (Book of the Arab Music Conference). Cairo: *al-Maṭbaᶜa al-Amīriyya.*

Laade, Wolfgang. 1962a. *Tunisia 1: The Classical Arab-Andalusian Music of Tunis*. Notes to FW 8861.

——. 1962c. *Tunisia 3: Folk Music*. Notes to FW 8863.

Louati, Ali. 1995. *Le Baron d'Erlanger et son Palais. Ennajma Ezzahra à Sidi Bou Said*. Tunis: Éditions Simpact.

El-Mahdi, Salah. n.d.a."Al-Nūba fi'l maghrib al-ᶜarbī" ("La Nawbah dans le maghreb arabe"). In a*l-Turāṯ* 3: 3–16.

——. n.d.b. "Al-Maqāmāt al-tūnisiyya al-muqarana" ("Étude Comparative des Modes Tunisiens.", In *al-Turāṯ* 8: 3–33.

——. n.d.c."Al-Īqāᶜāt al-mūsīqiyya al-ᶜarabiyya" ("Les Rhythmes dans la Musique Arabe"). In *al-Turāṯ* 9: 3–27.

——. n.d.d. [c. 1983]. *Maqāmāt al-mūsīqā al-ᶜarabiyya* (The *Maqāmāt* of Arab music). Tunis: *Našr al-Maᶜhad al-Rašīdī li-l-Mūsīqā al-Tūnisiyya.*

——. 1990. *Īqāᶜāt wa aškāl al-Mūsīqā al-ᶜArabiyya* (*Rythmes et Formes de la Musique Arabe*). Carthage: *Bayt al-Hikma Qartāj* (Fondation Nationale Carthage)

El-Mahdi, Salah and Mohamed Marzuqi. 1981. *Al-Ma'had al-rašīdī li-l-mūsīqā al-tūnisiyya* (the Rashidiyya Institute of Tunisian music). Tunis: *Wizārat al-Šu'ūn al-Taqāfiyya.*

Manuel, Peter. 1988. *Popular Musics of the Non-Western World: An Introductory Survey*. Oxford University Press.

Marcus, Scott. 1989. *Arab Music Theory in the Modern Period*. PhD diss. University of California, Los Angeles.

Moussali, Bernard. 1988. "Tunisia, Urban Music of Tunis." In *Congrès du Caire 1932: 145–51*. France: Édition Bibliothèque Nationale—l'Institut du Monde Arabe. Insert booklet to APN 88/9–10. Vols. 1&2.

——. 1992. "Les Premiers Enregistrements de Musique Tunisienne par les Compagnies Discographiques." Paper read at the inaugural program of the Centre des Musiques Arabes et Méditerranéennes, Gamarth, Tunisia, 9–12 November.

Powers, Harold S. 1980. "Classical Music, Cultural Roots and Colonial Rule: an Indic Musicologist looks at the Muslim World," *Asian Music* 12: 5–37.

Racy, Ali Jihad. 1981. "Music in Contemporary Cairo: a Comparative Overview," *Asian Music* 13/1: 4–21.

——. 1982. "Musical Aesthetics in Present-Day Cairo," *Ethnomusicology* 26/3: 391–406.

——. 1991. "Historical Worldviews of Early Ethnomusicologists: an East-West Encounter in Cairo, 1932." In Stephen Blum, Philip V. Bohlman, and Daniel M. Neuman., ed., *Ethnomusicology and Modern Music History*. Urbana & Chicago: University of Illinois Press.

Receuil des Travaux du Congrès de Musique Arabe. 1934. Cairo: Imprimerie Nationale, Boulac.

Rizgui, Sadok. 1967. *Al-Aġāni al-tūnisiyya* (Les Chants Tunisiens). Tunis: *al-dār al-Tūnisiyya li'l-Našr*.

Said, Rafik. 1970. *La Politique Culturelle en Tunisie*. Paris: UNESCO.

El-Shawan, Salwa. 1980."The Socio-Political Context of *Al-Musika Al-ᶜArabiyyah* in Cairo, Egypt: Policies, Patronage, Institutions, and Musical Change (1927–77). *Asian Music* 12/1: 86–128.

——. 1984. "Traditional Arab Music Ensembles in Egypt since 1967: 'The Continuity of Tradition within a Contemporary Framework?'", *Ethnomusicology* 28/2: 271–88.

Shakli, Mourad. 1994. *La Chanson Tunisienne. Analyse Technique et Approche Sociologique*. Thèse de Musicologie (Université de Paris-Sorbonne) Paris IV.

Snoussi, Mohamed. 1961. "Folklore Tunisien. Musique de Plein-Air. l'Orchestre de Tabbal et Zokkar," *Revue des Études Islamiques* 1:48–157.

Al-Turāṯ al-mūsīqī al-tunisi (*Patrimoine Musical Tunisien*). n.d. [Vol. 2: 1967]. 9 vols. Tunis: *Wizārat al-Šuʾūn al-Taqāfiyya*.

Yekta Bey, Rauf. 1922. "La Musique Turque." In Albert Lavignac, ed., *Encyclopédie de la Musique et Dictionnaire du Conservatoire* 1. Paris: Librerie Dalagrave.

Zbiss, Slimane-Mustafa. 1971. *Sidi Bou Said*. Tunis: Société Tunisienne de Diffusion.

Zghonda, Fethi. n.d. [c.1980]. *Al-mūsīqā al-nahasiyya fī tūnis* (*La Musique pour Harmonies en Tunisie*). Tunis. Wizārat al-Šuᶜūn at-Ṯaqāfiyya (Ministère des Affaires Culturelles).

———. 1994. Insert notes to *Tunisie Anthologie du Malouf. Musique Arabo-Andalouse. Nuba al-Sika*. Auvidis W 2600/59.

———. 1999. Insert notes to *Anthologie du Malouf Tunisien. La Nuba H'cin*. EE 002.

RECORDINGS

Unless otherwise noted, entries refer to compact discs. Entries arranged by date.

Musique Tunisienne, Enregistrements du Congrès du Caire. 1932. 20 discs, 78 rpm/25 cm, Gramophone HC 40–55 and HC 83–86.

Tunisia 1: The Classical Arab-Andalusian Music of Tunis. 1962a. Folkways Records FW 8861.

Tunisia 2: Religious Songs and Cantilations from Tunisia. 1962b. Folkways Records FW 8862.

Tunisia 3: Folk Music. 1962c. Folkways Records FW 8863.

Congrès du Caire 1932 2: Musique Citadine de Tlemcen/Algerie, Musique Savante de Fes/Maroc, Musique Citadine de Tunis/Tunisie. 1988. France: Édition Bibliotèque Nationale—l'Institut du Monde Arabe. APN 88-10.

Tunisie Anthologie du Malouf. Musique Arabo-Andalouse. Nuba al-Dhil. 1992. Orchestre et Chorale de la Radio Tunisienne, Direction: Abdelhamid Bel Eljia (Enregistrement historique: Tunis enr. mono 1959). Inédit, Auvidis W 260044.

Tunisie Anthologie du Malouf. Musique Arabo-Andalouse. Nuba al-Ramal. 1992. Orchestre et Chorale de la Radio Tunisienne, Direction: Abdelhamid Bel Eljia (Enregistrement historique: Tunis enr. mono 1960). Inédit, Auvidis W 260045.

Lotfi Boushnak: Malouf Tunisien. 1993. Maison des Cultures du Monde, Inédit, Auvidis W 260053.

Tunisie Anthologie du Malouf. Musique Arabo-Andalouse. Nuba al-Iraq. 1993. Orchestre et Chorale de la Radio Tunisienne, Direction, Abdelhamid Bel Eljia (Enregistrement historique: Tunis enr. mono 1960). Inédit, Auvidis W 260047.

Tunisie Anthologie du Malouf. Musique Arabo-Andalouse. Nuba al-Asbahan. 1993. Orchestre et Chorale de la Radio Tunisienne, Direction, Abdelhamid Bel Eljia (Enregistrement historique: Tunis enr. mono 1962). Inédit, Auvidis W 260046.

Tunisie Anthologie du Malouf. Musique Arabo-Andalouse. Nuba al-Sika. 1994. Ensemble de Musique Traditionelle de Tunis, Direction: Fethi Zghonda. Inédit, Auvidis W 260059.

Malouf Tunisien, La Musique Classique Tunisienne Congrès du Caire 1932. 1994. Artistes Arabes Associés—Club du Disque Arabe AAA 094.

El ᶜAzifet. n.d. [1998]. Direction Amina Srarfi. SOCA Music CD004.

Anthologie du Malouf Tunisien. La Nuba H'cin. 1999. Orchestre et Chorale de la Rachidia, Direction: Abdelhamid Belelgia, Ministère Tunisien de la Culture—Centre des Musiques Arabes et Méditerranénne—Ennejma Ezzehra, Distribution: Étranger: Sowarex / Bruxelles, EE 002.

Sonia M'Barek: Takht. 1999. World Network LC 6759.

Sonia M'Barek: Tawchih. 1999. Les Artistes Arabes Associés—Club du Disque Arabe AAA 186.

Salayha. n.d. SOCA MUSIC. CD 064.

Index

accordion, 99
aesthetics, vi 1, 37, 118
El Afrit, Cheikh (Issèrine Rozio), 119
aġānī. *See* compositional forms, definitions of: *uġniya*
al-āla, 2
Algeria, 2, 76, 95, 120n6. *See also* North Africa
Andalusian heritage, 42, 53, 71, 91, 97
Andalusian identity, vi, 2, 91–92
Andalusian refugees, vi, 2, 38, 75, 93
Arab accidental symbols, 12, 69n3
Arab Andalusian music, v, vi, 1–3
The Arab musical scale, 12
aristocratic patronage, 2, 4, 37–38, 42, 43, 44, 48, 51, 69n2, 91, 92
art music, 37, 91–92, 98
authenticity, viii, 55, 91, 100, 105, 108, 109, 110, 116, 118, 120n6
El ᶜAzifet, 118–19
ᶜAzūziyya, 97

Baghdad, 2, 103n8
bandir, 7
Bartók, Béla, 47
Belalgaied, Abdelkarim, 117–18
Belalgia, Abdelhamid, ix, 3, 55, 67, 68. *See also* personal interpretation
Ben Ali, Zine El Abidine, 105, 106, 119n1
Boudhina, Mohamed, 38, 39n7
Boughamha, Hamadi, ix, 43
Bourguiba, Habib, 75, 92, 105
Braham, Anouar, x
Bushnak, Lotfi, x, 16, 29, 40n9, 110, 112, 116–17

cafés, 4, 42, 44, 48, 77, 94, 111
Café M'rabbet, 42
Café des Nattes, 43, 50n3
The 1932 Cairo Congress, 14, 45,46, 47, 50, 50n4, 70n4, 97, 108, 110, 120n4
clarinet, 99
canon: notated, v–vi, 93, 99. *See also* *al-Turāṯ;* recorded, 99, 116
castanets, 119
celebrations, traditional, 4, 42, 77, 78, 79, 111, 118

About the Author

Ruth F. Davis is senior lecturer in ethnomusicology at the Universtiy of Cambridge and a fellow of Corpus Christi College Cambridge, where she directs studies in music. She has published and broadcast extensively in the fields of North African and Middle Eastern music.